CW01212874

# The Handbook of Work-based Pension Schemes

SECOND EDITION

# The Handbook of Work-based Pension Schemes

An employer's guide to designing and managing an effective pension scheme

Consultant editor: Adam Jolly

RECOMMENDED BY
INSTITUTE OF DIRECTORS

KoganPage

LONDON   PHILADELPHIA   NEW DELHI

**Publisher's note**
Every possible effort has been made to ensure that the information contained in this book is accurate at the time of going to press, and the publishers and authors cannot accept responsibility for any errors or omissions, however caused. No responsibility for loss or damage occasioned to any person acting, or refraining from action, as a result of the material in this publication can be accepted by the editor, the publisher or the authors.

First published by Kogan Page in 2013
Second edition 2016

Apart from any fair dealing for the purposes of research or private study, or criticism or review, as permitted under the Copyright, Designs and Patents Act 1988, this publication may only be reproduced, stored or transmitted, in any form or by any means, with the prior permission in writing of the publishers, or in the case of reprographic reproduction in accordance with the terms and licences issued by the CLA. Enquiries concerning reproduction outside these terms should be sent to the publishers at the undermentioned addresses:

| | | |
|---|---|---|
| 2nd Floor, 45 Gee Street | 1518 Walnut Street, Suite 1100 | 4737/23 Ansari Road |
| London | Philadelphia PA 19102 | Daryaganj |
| EC1V 3RS | USA | New Delhi 110002 |
| United Kingdom | | India |

© Kogan Page and individual contributors 2016

The right of Kogan Page to be identified as the author of this work has been asserted by him in accordance with the Copyright, Designs and Patents Act 1988.

ISBN    978 0 7494 7482 9
E-ISBN  978 0 7494 7483 6

The information in this book is correct as at November 2015.

**British Library Cataloguing-in-Publication Data**

A CIP record for this book is available from the British Library.

**Library of Congress Control Number**

2016934980

Typeset by Graphicraft Limited, Hong Kong
Print production managed by Jellyfish
Printed and bound in Great Britain by CPI Group (UK) Ltd, Croydon CR0 4YY by

# Challenging the status quo in Pension Law.

Dentons provides commercial and practical help to employers in managing their pension issues both in the UK and around the world. We work to shape pensions strategies that reflect your long-term business aims. We help with cost and risk management solutions and ensuring compliance with legal, regulatory and best practice requirements.

**Elmer Doonan**
Partner, London
D +44 20 7246 7151
elmer.doonan@dentons.com

**Jay Doraisamy**
Partner, London
D +44 20 7246 7574
jay.doraisamy@dentons.com

大成 DENTONS ▶ Know the way

dentons.com

©2016 Dentons. Dentons is a global legal practice providing client services worldwide through its member firms and affiliates. Please see dentons.com for Legal Notices.

# CONTENTS

## PART ONE  Pension challenges  1

**1.1**  The new retirement  3
*Malcolm Small, Retirement Income Alliance*

**1.2**  Wealth transfers  6
*Steve Lewis, LV= Corporate Solutions*

**1.3**  A pensions revolution  9
*Richard Butcher, PTL*

**1.4**  Reliefs and incentives  13
*Jeremy Goodwin*

## PART TWO  Framework for employers  19

**2.1**  Pensions for employers  21
*Mike Redston, Arc Benefits*

**2.2**  The legal background  30
*Roderick Ramage*

**2.3**  Automatic enrolment  35
*Roderick Ramage*

**2.4**  Other legal duties  38
*Roderick Ramage*

**2.5**  Other legal options  42
*Roderick Ramage*

## PART THREE  Scheme choices  47

**3.1** Scheme creation for small employers  49
*Elmer Doonan, Dentons*

**3.2** The pensions landscape  53
*Dean Wetton*

**3.3** International pension plans  57
*Carl Hansen, BWCI*

## PART FOUR  Legacy and recovery  61

**4.1** Pension restructuring  63
*Elmer Doonan, Dentons*

**4.2** Legacy options  69
*Guy Freeman, Rothesay Life*

**4.3** DB transfers  75
*Steve Lewis, LV= Corporate Solutions*

**4.4** Insured solutions  78
*Guy Freeman, Rothesay Life*

## PART FIVE  Scheme design  83

**5.1** How to integrate everyone into a coherent scheme  85
*Carole Nicholls, Nicholls Stevens*

**5.2** Pensions for top performers  93
*Ronald Olufunwa, Westminster Wealth*

**5.3** How to set up an international scheme  103
*Carl Hansen, BWCI*

## PART SIX  Risk management  107

**6.1** Risks for scheme sponsors  109
*Richard Butcher, PTL*

**6.2** Systems and processes  113
*Bob Compton, Arc Benefits*

**6.3** Employee risks  120
*Steve Lewis, LV= Corporate Solutions*

## PART SEVEN  Investment strategy  127

**7.1** De-risking investments  129
*Dean Wetton*

**7.2** Investments and assets  133
*Dean Wetton*

**7.3** Performance and value  136
*Dean Wetton*

**7.4** VAT recovery  140
*Elmer Doonan, Dentons*

# PART ONE
# Pension challenges

# The new retirement

## 1.1

*The rise of senior entrepreneurs reflects profound changes in how pensions now work, says Malcolm Small, chairman of the Retirement Income Alliance and former senior policy adviser at the Institute of Directors.*

Directors are re-engaging with pensions. They are already taking the lead in extending pensions to all their workers and they are reimagining how their own careers might unfold. As employers, all of them are now being drawn into the process of signing up their employees to schemes at work. Over the next two years, directors in 850,000 smaller companies will find themselves facing the challenge of creating and managing schemes. It is likely to be a tougher challenge than many of them imagine.

At the same time, all directors will be working out the implications of the biggest change in pensions than any of us can remember: the freedom for anyone to take the fund they have accumulated by the time they reach 55, then spend it, invest it or pass it on, as they see fit.

All such calculations will soon be taken in light of likely changes in reliefs in tax for pension contributions. In principle, few would dispute that a country with a deficit as large as ours can keep deferring billions in revenue each year. The question is how to put an alternative in place without undermining the system as a whole.

Taken together, these three big changes in our pensions systems mean that we will all start thinking about retirement in new ways. The old model when you stopped work and went on one long holiday is disappearing fast.

For directors personally, it is how they would prefer to lead their lives anyway. As a matter of choice, few expect to stop work any time soon. They would like to scale back and control their own schedule. Many expect to start their own businesses.

A typical model is to start drawing on their pension in their late 50s and early 60s, begin perhaps two to three ventures, act as a mentor to younger talent, then start contributing to their pensions again once a business is up and running. They will only then draw on their pension again in their 70s, although many IoD members never expect to stop working at all.

To some, it might appear a risky way to retire. For many, it means that they will earn more as older entrepreneurs than they did in their earlier careers. For others, it is a way of keeping themselves sharp and engaged. No-one wants to be the executive who retires only to fall ill or die within months.

## Schemes at work

Overall, retirement is changing out of all recognition. The over-65s are the fastest-growing cohort of employees in the UK and 7 per cent of the over-70s are in work. Few can stop work at 60 and then live comfortably to 95. The whole shape of retirement as we have historically understood it is changing.

Employers are waking up to the realization that if they want to have a conversation about when someone is going to retire, it has to be economically possible. The state pension is reasonable, but on its own most will choose to continue working to supplement their income.

Instead, workplace schemes can put everyone in a much stronger position. Between them, employers and employees should ideally be contributing 15 per cent of earnings year in, year out. The current standard is half that level at best.

So far, the evidence is that employees will manage the funds that they accumulate responsibly. The fear that they would buy fast cars or take exotic holidays looks largely misplaced. They realize that it is the only asset they have to support themselves for the rest of their lives. So any expenditure is generally sensible: paying off a mortgage, settling debts, supporting their children.

The experience of employers in automatically enrolling all their employees in a workplace scheme has been mixed. Large employers have progressively taken on this responsibility since 2012. The reports are that the process has been more time consuming, more expensive and more difficult than anyone originally thought. It has proved a complex task to work through the rules on who to include and what proportion of their earnings qualify.

Originally, the worry was that the volume of employees could overwhelm the system. In late 2014 a breakdown was narrowly avoided. Now the worry is about the volume of smaller employers who are due to join the system during the course of 2016–17.

Many are leaving it late and could well come to grief. Unlike larger employers, they do not have departments for HR and finance to whom they can turn. The pensions regulator is trying to simplify the process as far as possible and a number of multi-employer funds are now well established.

Nest is the government's default fund. Other mastertrusts, such as Now, the People's Pension, Standard Life and Legal & General, are designed to simplify the demands on how risks are governed. However, not all are in the market for smaller companies and the minimum charge for employers may prove too high.

Alternatively, smaller companies can take out a contract for a group personal pension plan through one of the insurers, although it will demand a higher level of compliance.

One option on which to exercise caution will be services from smaller master-trusts and investment advisers. The fear is that a lack of oversight could open up the potential for extensive fraud.

Instead of doing the minimum, employers could take the initiative and create their own scheme through one of the numerous strong propositions from investment managers. They could resolve to do better than the rules and keep it simple by putting everyone who works for them into a scheme as a condition of employment. The employee could contribute 5 per cent of total earnings and employees could do the same. Such a scheme would automatically comply with the regulator and sidestep a lot of complications.

## Future of relief

Even so, two further questions are fast looming. Both revolve round tax.

Pensions have long depended on the relief given to contributions. In total, it is estimated to benefit employers and employees by £52bn a year. Why not simplify the system to bring this revenue forward for the government and strengthen the confidence of those who are saving for their retirement?

So we are likely to see lower levels of relief and, more radically, a switch towards a 'retirement ISA', which is a model that employees already understand and which could encourage them to push up the level of their contributions. It would probably be introduced as a parallel system to test whether it could offer an alternative to existing schemes.

For most businesses, any switch would represent a simple transfer of value from schemes whose value depends on the level of contributions. In the public sector, which operates unfunded schemes based on final salaries, it would be certain to cause any outcry. So far, no-one has shown any willingness to grasp the nettle of managing the government's £1.4 trillion in pension liabilities.

More immediately, directors are tempering their enthusiasm for their new freedom in the use of their own retirement savings by the limits on how much they can contribute. The allowance each year is down from £220,000 to £40,000 and over their career is restricted to £1m. It seems an unfortunate disincentive for those who are otherwise ready to back new ventures and future growth in their second, third and fourth careers.

For further details, see www.riaonline.co.uk

# Wealth transfers

## 1.2

*Freedom and choice in pensions is transforming personal expectations of pensions, says Steve Lewis at LV= Corporate Solutions.*

The pension changes announced in the 2014 budget prompted the biggest change to pension legislation in generations. Leading economic consultant Michael Burke called it 'the biggest financial experiment ever undertaken'. For the first time since private pensions were introduced, it is now possible for individuals to withdraw as much cash as they require from their defined contribution (DC) pensions without the legal requirement to also have a level of secured pension income that is sustainable for the rest of their life.

The budget also dramatically changed the wealth transfer opportunities. In most cases pension funds can now be passed on to any dependant or nominated beneficiary completely free of tax if the pensioner dies before age 75, or at the beneficiary's marginal rate of tax if the pensioner dies after the age of 75. Unsurprisingly, these rules make DC pensions a very attractive saving and inheritance tax planning vehicle for many employees – and not just the very wealthy.

## New challenges for members, sponsors and trustees

The significantly increased attractiveness of the DC pension is likely to result in many scheme members with benefits within defined benefits (DB) schemes to assess whether they should transfer their benefits from DB to DC. This will also inevitably lead to increased challenges for scheme trustees, who will be faced with reconciling the requests from members with their duty-of-care to ensure the best retirement outcomes.

> The challenge for all responsible sponsors who operate a DB pension scheme is to have a clear and robust process that is fair to all and supports the best outcomes for the member.

The majority of members will have saved relatively small amounts in their DC arrangements and therefore the allure of a potentially large amount of money to spend as they choose and pass onto their beneficiaries free of tax will be very appealing. It has been well documented by many research bodies that human beings have a very strong inherent 'present bias' ie people place more value on 'money now' than the promise of 'money in the future'. With current transfer values averaging at 25-30 times the pension benefit, even a relatively modest DB benefit will generate a significant transfer value. This presents the majority of people with a challenge of making the right decision over what to do with a potentially life-changing sum. For example a £5,000 DB benefit could provide a transfer value of over £100,000. These are sums of money which members could not previously have imagined being able to access and with the new rules and the government publicity promoting the DC pension as a bank account, this may be an attraction too difficult to reject.

## Understanding the choices – and the risks

Although the new flexibility and wealth transfer opportunities may make a transfer more appropriate for many people, the process shifts a significant amount of risk to the member. Risks, which many customers do not understand. For example, it's widely accepted that members are likely to underestimate how long they will live and over estimate the investment return they will receive in retirement. The trends in Australia and America provide an interesting insight here as these two countries have enjoyed 'pension freedoms' for some time now. Their experiences show that nearly 25 per cent of Australians have exhausted their funds by the age of 70 while it's estimated that half of Americans in retirement will outlive their funds.* In Australia the current debate about reintroducing compulsory annuitization shows the concern and the extent to which members have misunderstood the risks of ruin.

## Getting the right process in place

Historically, the industry and the regulator have, quite rightly, been cautious about DB transfers. Although this caution remains, there is a growing acceptance that, for a large minority of scheme members, a transfer from DB to a DC environment might be in their best interests. Although there's no overall agreement on likely numbers, two prominent Employee Benefit Consultants (EBCs) have publicly estimated that

*Source: Pensions policy institute (update 66)

between 30 per cent to 40 per cent are likely to transfer their DB benefits. Discussions with trustees and EBCs suggest that this number could be increased significantly if the scheme offers partial transfers. If correct, in addition to the wider duty-of-care considerations faced by the trustees, this would increase the complexity and cost of providing transfer values and place increased administrative strain on the scheme. The significant, beneficial impact on the scheme sponsor transferring pension liabilities to the member has the potential to create a conflict of interest. The challenge for all responsible sponsors who operate a DB pension scheme is therefore to have a clear and robust process that is fair to all and supports the best outcomes for the member. Given the lack of understanding of the risks involved and the temptation presented by access to potentially large sums of cash, scheme members will need support and guidance to educate them about their options to ensure we do not experience similar statistics as Australia and America in the future.

> As the Head of Distribution, Steve Lewis is a member of the LV= Retirement Solutions leadership team that has transformed the business over the last five years from being a niche annuity provider to a mainstream retirement business. The delivery of new propositions to market has been a key focus of his work, particularly through the transformation of the market resulting from the introduction of pension freedoms. LV= has been at the forefront of technology developments, providing client education and adviser support tools, and now launching groundbreaking on-line education and advice tools. Steve is a retirement specialist with considerable industry experience, working closely with advisers and providers in the market. To find out more about LV= Corporate Solutions and how they can help you, call the LV= Corporate Solutions team on 08000 850 260, email Corporate.Solutions@lv.com or visit LV.com/corporatesolutions

# A pensions revolution

1.3

*Richard Butcher at PTL reviews how the ensions industry is reacting to the most radical and unexpected shake-up in living memory.*

In his March 2014 Budget, the Chancellor of the Exchequer shocked the pension industry by announcing changes to the private pension system that some later described as the most radical since the 1920s.

Leaving aside the hyperbole, what did he do, what impact will the changes have and what risks do they create for companies?

How the pension system changed

Until April 2015 an employee in a workplace defined contribution (DC) pension scheme had very few options at retirement.

They had to use their accumulated pot of money to provide an income (except for 25 per cent of the pot which could be taken as tax free cash) either through a 'drawdown' product where they drew money straight from the pot subject to HMRC limits which were designed to avoid it being exhausted, or purchasing an annuity; a retail financial product based on an insurance policy that paid an income for life.

In addition, employees in trust-based schemes (ie those set up under trust as opposed to contract-based schemes' like group personal pension plans) often had to have the consent of their employer to take their pot.

George Osborne liberalized all of this.

Since April any member over the age of 55, with or without the consent of their employer, has been free to take their entire pot as cash with the element above 25 per cent taxed as earned income in the year that it is paid. Many employees have taken their pots as a one off cash payment, while others are taking them in tranches to reduce tax liability. The government also allowed two new payment mechanisms: one to allow the tax free cash to be paid upfront and the other to allow it to be drawn out as a percentage of each payment. The net result of these liberalization to date, is that approximately £2.8bn (source: ABI) of assets have been taken from pensions savings.

## What impact will the changes have?

The changes were launched under a banner of giving people the freedom to determine their own financial future. They would, the Chancellor said, be put in control of and trusted with their own money.

Many in the industry characterized the policy as a punt; it might work, creating more informed and engaged consumers and better value products, or it might equally fail catastrophically, creating a generation of 'retirees' partying on cruise ships with brand new cars waiting dockside, before falling back on the State when the cash runs out. What will happen in practice remains to be seen, however, early evidence is encouraging; a relatively small proportion of the over 55 population have taken their pot (forecast as 20 per cent in the first year) and many of those that do use the money sensibly, often to pay down debt.

The Freedom ad Choice policy was so radical that it was launched without any evidence on how employees and consumers would behave (similar models do exist elsewhere in the world, most notably Australia and Switzerland, although their experiences often conflict with each other). It was also launched, because of the impact that it would have on the share prices of the insurers writing large volumes of annuity business, without any industry consultation. Less obviously, the changes challenged the pension providers to develop better value retirement products. In particular, the Chancellor had in his sights, the annuity market which was perceived to offer poor value.

In this respect, again, whether this will work remains to be seen. The lead into the change in the law was too short for the providers to build new products that would be robust enough to withstand the often retrospective scrutiny of financial regulators, although, again, early signs are encouraging.

Finally, the policy had one other intent, the success of which has far exceeded expectations. By allowing pots to be paid as taxed cash, the treasury has reaped a windfall of hundreds of millions of pounds.

## What are the risks to businesses?

So the early signs are that the changes seem to work for members, seem to have changed the financial market for the better and have definitely reaped a windfall for the Treasury. All good.

Or are there risks that have been ignored?

Putting aside the fact that the evidence of consumer and market behaviour is still early evidence there is a section of the pension infrastructure that has so far been ignored: employers.

Private companies have been providing pensions since the 18th century, although they only became widespread during the 20th. Originally the intention was largely altruistic: they wanted to look after the people (usually the senior ones) who had given them many years of their lives, to protect them against an impoverished old age. Later, as workplace pensions became mainstream, the motive changed. During the mid-20th century production lines could only operate at the speed of the slowest operative. A pension was a way of removing the older slower worker, so that they could be replaced with a younger faster worker. In the later part of the 20th century, pension schemes were used as a tool to help companies rationalize their workforce in the face of rapidly advancing technology. Around the same time, public perception of retirement was changing. No longer was it being 'put out to grass'; instead it was a 'long holiday', 20 years of relative health and wealth and the resultant opportunities. In this environment, pensions became a recruitment and retention tool. In other words, companies provided pensions as a way to manage people into a business, to keep them in the business and then, later, to manage them out of the business as they became economically less viable.

The pension reforms make it more difficult to achieve the last of these objectives.

## Jimmy's story

Madeup Ltd manufactures and fits plastic roofing. The manufacturing process involves heavy machinery and the fitting process requires heavy work often at heights. Average earnings are relatively low, but slightly above the sector average. It provides a DC scheme to its staff and pays a generous (for the sector) 8 per cent employer contribution. The staff pay nothing. By happy coincidence, they find out later, this contribution plus the state pension means that their average employee will retire with an income equivalent to the government estimated amount necessary for an adequate retirement.

Jimmy has worked for Madeup since he left school. He has done well, rising to team supervisor by his mid 50s. The days of him having to lug gear up ladders have passed, but he occasionally finds he has to fill in for a fitter if they are ill. His is a tough physical job.

In 2016 Jimmy's wife, Jo, became seriously ill. She recovered, but the experience shocked them and changed their outlook. They felt young, but they realized they may not live forever. More practically, because Jo had to stop work for close to a year, they struggled with money, running up arrears on their mortgage and debt on their credit cards.

Jimmy had heard of the pension freedoms and rang the pension scheme. To cut a long story short, he took all of the cash. To reduce the tax liability he took it in three payments: the first to pay of their immediate debts and a chunk of the mortgage, the second to pay the rest of the mortgage and the third, well, to have some fun. A holiday of a lifetime in Portugal and the new, albeit modest, car Jimmy had always wanted.

That car lasted Jimmy ten years. He sold it just days before the HR manager asked him to pop by.

'Jimmy,' he said after the pleasantries, 'you're a good man and you've done sterling work for the company, but you're no spring chicken. Climbing ladders and hefting stuff is a young man's job. Have you thought about retirement?'

'Geoff,' he replied, 'I have and I'd love to but, well, I can't. I'm a bit embarrassed to tell you this but I've already spent my pension money. I've no choice, I've got to stay on and keep earning.'

The pension freedoms, combined with the abolition of compulsory retirement ages, mean that companies can no longer manage people out of their business. Indeed, it means they can no longer even rely on their employees using the contributions that the company has paid to provide for old age. The employer can't stop them from using those contributions to pay off debt, have the holiday of a lifetime or buy a sports car.

## So what can the employer do?

On the face of it, there's little that an employer can do to mitigate this risk; it's too new and uncertain for mitigation tools to have been developed. That said, there are some ideas floating around albeit, at this stage untried and untested. One of these is that an employer holds money (above the minimum pension contribution) in a bare trust or even on their balance sheet and uses it tactically to help employees exit the business. This wouldn't be as efficient as a traditional pension scheme but, then again, neither is a modern pension scheme.

The pension freedoms may or may not be a good thing for employees. They, however, are most certainly not a good thing for employers. Ask Geoff.

---

Richard Butcher is Managing Director of PTL, a firm that provides professional pension governance services to other companies. He is Chair of the PLSA's DC Council and sits on their board. He is also on the council of the PMI and a member of the DWP trustees panel and TPR's Dc practitioner panel.

# Reliefs and incentives

**1.4**

*Since George Osborne's March 2014 Budget, the pension tax regime has undergone major changes, with more to come. Jeremy Goodwin summarizes what you really need to know.*

## Already here – new retirement options

The real headline-grabbing news was the new flexibilities relating to money purchase pension benefits, which were introduced at the start of the 2015–16 tax year.

From 6 April 2015, when taking their pension benefits, all money purchase pension savers can (if the terms of their pension plan allow it) choose from the following new benefit options:

- **Flexi-access drawdown,** under which the pension pot remains invested, with the member being able to draw sums from it which are flexible as to amount and timing. Previously, drawdown was restricted to those with larger pension pots or the amount which could be drawn was capped, but no such legal restrictions apply to the new model of drawdown (though pension providers may impose some restrictions).
- Taking pension purely as one or more cash lump sums (the new **'uncrystallized funds pension lump sum'** or **UFPLS**).
- **Flexible annuities,** the amount of which can go down as well as up (unlike standard lifetime annuities).

In addition, the familiar options of (standard) annuity purchase or payment of a scheme pension from an occupational pension plan remain available.

In all cases, the saver is currently able to benefit from the usual 25 per cent tax-free cash amount. This can be taken upfront when using drawdown, when buying an annuity (whether flexible or standard) or when a scheme pension is payable. If taking benefits as one or more UFPLS payments, 25 per cent of each cash lump sum is payable tax-free.

## Already here – new options for death benefits

Alongside these changes, 6 April 2015 also saw equally radical changes to the taxation of benefits paid where the pension saver dies leaving unused money purchase pension savings. These unused savings may either be 'uncrystallized' funds (where the saver has not yet accessed their benefits at the date of death) or undrawn funds held in a flexi-access drawdown arrangement.

In broad terms, there are now the same options for payment of death benefits from these unused savings as there are for retirement benefits. This includes, in particular, the options of payment as a cash lump sum or in the form of a beneficiary's annuity or beneficiary's drawdown.

However, in an unexpectedly generous change, if death benefits from unused savings are taken in any of the three forms just listed, the resulting benefits will be payable entirely free of income tax where the pension saver dies below age 75. To qualify for this beneficial treatment, the beneficiary's drawdown arrangement/annuity must be set up, or the lump sum must be paid, within two years of the date when the scheme administrator first knows (or ought reasonably to have known) of the saver's death.

If the pension saver is aged 75 or over at the date of death, or if the beneficiary's drawdown arrangement/annuity is set up outside that two-year window, pension income payable from that arrangement or annuity is taxable at the recipient's marginal rate. For the 2015–16 tax year, the treatment for lump sums paid in such circumstances is slightly different (a fixed 45 per cent tax rate will be applied), but the intention is for these lump sums also to be taxed at the recipient's marginal rate from 6 April 2016. This is a major change, since lump sum payments payable on death at age 75 (or from drawdown arrangements at any age) were previously subject to a hefty tax charge of 55 per cent .

Equivalent rules apply to the taxation of pension income to a beneficiary where the pension saver uses his money purchase pension pot at retirement to buy a joint life annuity or a guaranteed annuity and then dies before age 75, though in that case there is no requirement for any action to be taken within the two-year window (since the beneficiary's annuity already exists). However, where an occupational pension plan pays a scheme pension directly to a beneficiary, that pension income will continue to be taxable at the recipient's marginal rate, regardless of the pension saver's age at death: an odd quirk.

Another important change is that any unused money purchase funds which are left to a beneficiary can continue to be passed on upon the beneficiary's subsequent death, with essentially the same tax rules applying (by reference to the beneficiary's age at death). Previously, there was very limited scope for this kind of inter-generational transfer of unused pension savings.

And in another new departure, the pension saver or beneficiary can nominate any person as the intended recipient, rather than payments being restricted to spouses, children or other financial dependants. At present, there is a risk that, if this nomination is made legally binding, there may be an inheritance tax liability in some cases, but HMRC has confirmed that the intention is also to remove that risk.

## Already here – £10,000 annual allowance cap on money purchase savings

From 6 April 2015, there is a new £10,000 allowance for money purchase savings where an individual has opted to access money purchase benefits through one of the new flexible options described above (or in certain other limited scenarios).

This new restricted allowance is an anti-avoidance measure, intended to curb income tax evasion under which savers could set up a salary sacrifice arrangement with their employer to contribute to a money purchase plan, from which regular UFPLS (with a 25 per cent tax-free element) are then drawn in place of employment income. If the saver also has defined benefit savings, these are separately tested against the £30,000 balance of the standard annual allowance.

## Coming up – cuts to lifetime allowance

As well as the £10,000 cap just described, there are to be further reductions to limits on tax-relieved savings. Already cut to £1.25m at the start of the 2014–15 tax year, the lifetime allowance will fall again to £1m from 6 April 2016. Longer term, the intention is that the lifetime allowance will be indexed by reference to increases in CPI from April 2018, and so should start to rise.

The Government has promised transitional protection for those who have already built up benefits above the £1m ceiling as at April 2016, similar to the various forms of protection introduced alongside previous changes to the lifetime allowance, such as enhanced protection and fixed protection. Full details of these protections are still awaited at the time of writing.

## Coming up – restriction of pensions tax relief for high earners

The July 2015 Budget confirmed the (widely predicted) restriction of pensions tax relief for high earners, with the introduction of a tapered annual allowance from

6 April 2016. Tapering will start where an individual's adjusted income, calculated before deduction of member contributions and including the value of employer contributions, is at least £150,000. The standard allowance of £40,000 will be reduced by £1 for every £2 of income above the £150,000 threshold, down to a minimum allowance of £10,000 for those with adjusted income of £210,000 or above. The test relates to income, not just earnings, and therefore it may well be difficult for pension savers to predict whether or not they will be caught by the tapering provisions.

Individuals whose income is £110,000 or less (before adding in the value of pension contributions) are not caught by the tapering provisions. However, there are anti-avoidance measures which mean that any post-9 July 2015 salary sacrifice arrangements relating to pension contributions must be disregarded when applying this threshold test.

## On the horizon – all change?

Not content with the above changes, in his July 2015 Budget the Chancellor also announced a wide-ranging review of the entire system of pensions tax relief, as set out in HM Treasury's paper, Strengthening the incentive to save: a consultation on pensions tax relief, issued on 8 July 2015. The consultation period closed on 30 September 2015.

In the consultation paper, HMT invited views on how the current system of tax relief might be changed so as to encourage higher levels of pension saving, whilst still remaining fiscally sustainable over the longer-term. Apart from changes to the lifetime allowance and annual allowance, the only reform option specifically mentioned in the paper was the possibility of moving to a system of upfront taxation, where income tax is charged at the point contributions are placed into the pensions savings vehicle rather than when pension benefits are ultimately drawn by the saver.

The implications for pension providers and savers of such a change would be huge. For example, it is not at all clear what tax treatment would apply to benefits which have already been built up under the old system. The normal approach in these cases would be to ring-fence those existing benefits and administer them under the old tax system, but this would make the already complex system even more complicated.

Other options which have been discussed during the debate triggered by the consultation paper include:

- introduction of flat-rate tax relief, set at a level above basic rate but below higher rate
- adoption of the model used in Ireland of a stamp-duty style tax on all pension savings
- capping or removing the entitlement to tax-free cash

All of these would have significant consequences for pension savers, and for employers considering the optimal design for the remuneration package they offer to employees.

At the time of writing, it is not clear what (if anything) HMT plans to do in response to the consultation, although industry commentators, employers, trustees and pension providers have consistently pleaded for any further changes to be carefully considered, and introduced at a much more moderate pace than was the case with all the recent developments listed above.

## Action points

Any employer which provides a money purchase pension plan needs to think about the following key points:

- **Which (if any) of the new retirement and death benefit options should be available from its plan?** It is not currently mandatory to provide direct access to these new flexibilities. The employer's preferred options will need to be discussed with the plan trustees (for an occupational pension plan) or provider (for a contract-based arrangement such as a group personal pension plan).
- **Will providing options such as flexi-access drawdown expose the employer or trustees to complaints if the retired employee (or beneficiary) runs out of pension savings?** This could arise as a result of over-spending, or because of poor investment returns during the drawdown period. Where this is a concern, an obvious alternative is to provide access to such products only through transfer to an external provider which specializes in these arrangements.
- **Should access to UFPLS be restricted?** The idea of savers being able to use their pension pot like an ATM is not popular, because of the administrative costs associated with making cash payments (for example, the need to operate PAYE on each payment). Appropriate restrictions on the number, size and frequency of cash payments are definitely something to consider.

The employer's policy on these points will also need to be kept under review, as market practice is still evolving rapidly (as is the availability of commercial retirement products offering access to these new options).

All employers also need to think about what, if anything, they intend to do to assist high earners who may be caught by the reduced lifetime allowance or by the new tapered annual allowance. For instance, should the employer look at capping contributions or pensionable pay for affected individuals? Should a requirement for matching employee contributions be waived, if this will enable the employee to get full value from the employer contributions without suffering a tax charge?

Finally, employers need to keep a watching brief on longer-term developments in this area. If HMT does decide that the fiscal lure of a switch to upfront taxation is impossible to resist, employers may need radically to rethink their pensions offering to employees.

---

Jeremy specializes in a wide range of pensions law issues, including: trustees' responsibilities and duties, the Regulator's anti-avoidance powers, pension aspects of both corporate transactions and debt finance, investment-related matters, and all other matters arising from establishing pension schemes to winding them up.

Jeremy's experience includes advice on: various pension scheme mergers, establishing various final salary, career average revalued earnings, and money purchase pension schemes (including where sectionalized for funding purposes), investment management and custody agreements, and the closure of schemes to future accrual and the adoption of money purchase benefits for future service.

Jeremy is a full member of the Association of Pension Lawyers, and is on its Legislative and Parliamentary Committee. Jeremy is also a member of the Pensions Management Institute (PMI), and was awarded the Retirement Provision Diploma in July 2005. He is a member of the PMI committee responsible for the APMI qualification, and drafts the material for the law module. His articles are regularly published in the pensions press, and he often talks at conferences and seminars. Further details: jeremygoodwin@eversheds.com

# PART TWO
# Framework for employers

# ARC
## Benefits Limited

## Pensions Management & Governance Specialists

**Hindsight**……is usually a regret…..and often comes at great cost……

**Foresight**…is usually the preserve of the unsung hero…requiring thought and implementation..

**Insight**………..is usually highly valued by those that need to know…

**Focus ARC's expertise on your Pensions Management and Governance**

Oakfield House, 478 Station Road, Dorridge, West Midlands, B93 8HE  **01564 775877**
www.arcbenefits.co.uk     email: bob.compton@arcbenefits.co.uk

# Pensions for employers

## 2.1

*Mike Redston at Arc Benefits reviews how employers can best manage their responsibilities, liabilities and risks.*

In the UK, the structure for providing pensions has become unnecessarily complex, but at its very simplest, the objective for employers should be no different now from what it was originally: to *put aside some money now for workers to access when too old to work.*

The moral responsibility therefore is to do what's fair for the employees without unacceptable detriment to the business, and in such a way that makes best use of the money in the interim without undue risk. Easier said than done but this involves:

- Deciding what is affordable and fair (design)
- Choosing and putting in place the means of delivery (the scheme)
- Ensuring information is accurate and clear (data and communication)
- Appointing reliable people and organizations to carry out the required functions (the mechanics)
- Monitoring the full range of activities to ensure all is going well (Governance)

In a nutshell this is the pensions management function that all good employers should be addressing whether or not the business is big enough to warrant its own pensions manager.

This article covers some of the things for employers and Directors to think about including some questions for your own consideration to help you assess how you stand and help identify what may need looking into.

## The legal minimum

Every employer has a responsibility to take pensions seriously. Even the smallest will have to make work-based pension provision for qualifying workers. Company

Boards and business owners have a responsibility to know the date applicable to their business (the 'staging date') and ensure everything is dealt with accurately and on time. Find out your 'staging date' and take action to avoid breaking the law and risk of penalty.

This has loosely been called auto-enrolment or 'AE', but there is more to it than that.

- Some workers have to be entered into a scheme automatically (but may opt out).
- Others have a right to request membership.
- For those who opt out, there are subsequent rights for automatic re-enrolment.

All of these practicalities need care. It is illegal to manipulate your workforce to avoid these obligations.

For legal compliance, there are technical definitions as to what constitutes a 'worker' and eligibility rules based on earnings and age apply, with timescales then applicable for carrying out certain processes. Whilst knowing the broad rules is a good starting point, the detail at a functional level could be very specific to your business. For example, some businesses may have different payrolls for different categories of employee and various components of pay (basic, overtime, bonus, shift allowance, sick pay, maternity/paternity leave etc). Add to this the potential grey areas (contract workers, secondments, overseas workers , non executive directors etc.) and you will understand that there is a need for employers to be able to identify with certainty who is affected and when.

- What is your staging date?
- Do you know how many 'workers' (as defined by law) you have in total?
    - If you have passed your staging date, do you know:
    - how many people have been automatically enrolled?
    - how many people have opted out?
    - how many are not entitled to auto enrolment but have requested to join?
    - the date when any opt outs have to be automatically rejoined?

At the smaller end of the market (micro employers), there is now to be a requirement to declare where auto enrolment does not apply, for example where there are low paid casual workers. The purpose here seems to be the need for certainty that every employer (and this even includes domestic situations eg nannies, a care worker or gardener) doesn't wriggle out of the obligations. All a bit heavy handed, but morally there are still issues. Why shouldn't a person with several part time jobs have the same access to pension savings as someone earning the same amount with one employer?

## Types of pension scheme

The employer needs to decide how the obligation will be delivered. There are two broad types of pension scheme:

- **defined contribution:** you define what is paid into a scheme but not what comes out
- **defined benefit:** you make a promise of what you will pay on retirement (usually by formula). The risk to the employer is that you don't know what the ultimate cost will be

There are some schemes with a bit of both (hybrid).

Beyond this, there are further options for the employer as to whether to have its own trust-based scheme or be adhered to a broader type of scheme that can deal with many employers (eg a master trust).

## Defined contribution schemes

Most new schemes will be of the defined contribution type. There are minimum levels of contribution required by law but you may choose more. These are effectively savings schemes with you as the employer making sure the levels of contribution are clearly defined (usually split between employer and employee) and what levels of earnings these percentages are applied to. Whilst there are numerous investment possibilities, the big legal principle is that schemes used for auto enrolment purposes must have in place a default investment structure that will apply where individuals do not make a choice otherwise. There are maximum levels of charging that must apply to these defaults.

- How many defined contribution pension schemes do you operate for future contribution purposes?
- What is the legal structure for these (ymaster trustour own trust, master trust, contract-based)?
- What is the formula for contributions (standard for all, variable percentages)?
- What is the formula for determining pensionable earnings?
- How many investment options are available? How many members have opted for an investment structure other that the default?

## Defined benefit schemes

Because of the promises, this can be a financial risk to an employer. The Employer needs to know what schemes it has (old schemes can still be incurring costs!) and manage them as efficiently as possible. It is extremely important for the employer to know the status of each scheme:

- Who is the principle employer of the scheme?
- Which other employers adhere to the scheme?
- Is it still open to new joiners?
- Are members still accruing future service benefits?
- Is it running as closed scheme?
- Is it totally wound up etc?
- What is the funding position (in deficit/in surplus)?

These types of schemes must be trust-based. There can be different ways of operating a trust. Individuals could be classified as 'member representatives', 'independent trustee' or 'employer representatives'. There could be a trust company with the individuals appointed as Directors of that trust company; this company could be independent of the employer or a company within your group. The employer needs to be very clear of the trustee structure applicable, who the officers are and how they were appointed etc, but regardless of this it is very important to be clear what the trust deeds and rules specify regarding powers and responsibilities (employer only, trustee only or joint); for trust companies, the memoranda and articles of association will also be relevant.

Regardless of the structure, the trustees have obligations to the employer and vice versa. Unless managed sensibly, there can be uncomfortable situations with trustees in battle with sponsoring employers or employers letting the trustees get on with it without much control (and the poor pensions manager stuck in the middle!). The crux of the matter is usually what is called the 'employer covenant'; how strong is the company's ability to support the funding? Where exactly in a bigger group is this funding supported? There may be conflicts of interest and confidentiality issues but constructive discussion between the employer and trustees is far better than confrontation.

One specific issue relevant to defined benefit schemes that should have been dealt with relates to the ability to contract-out of the state scheme. This ceases from 6 April 2016. In a broader context, the solvency and funding of defined benefit schemes can be a major risk and worry. There are means of managing liabilities away from the employer and some Employers may wish to consider these.

- How many defined benefit schemes relate to you as an employer? What is the status of these?
- How are trustees appointed and how do they interact with the employer?
- Does the employer have strategy on dealing with defined benefit schemes going forward?

## Related benefit schemes and discretions and insurances

There needs to be a full understanding of discretionary practices as opposed to rights. Rights by definition should be clearly defined. For discretions, there firstly needs to be a right to be considered and then a judgement; things such as early retirement, ill health provision, dependants' pensions, children's pensions, and pension increases can fall into this category and sometimes expensive practices can build up. These may be the right things to do but there is a need to ensure these are subject to the correct control processes. There could also be pension related matters outside of pension scheme documentation (eg a practice or commitment to pension enhancements on termination or redundancy).

There are also some allied complications to look out for. Whilst it is common to have life assurance provision associated with a pension scheme, this may need to be run as a separate scheme. There may also be other aspects such as employers' liability or director liability insurance which may be relevant to pensions aspects, and trustee directors etc. Rather than looking at pensions in isolation, it is worth looking at the fuller picture within contracts and terms of employment and insurances to ensure other related benefit provisions (salary sacrifice, medical insurance, sick pay etc.) are still logical for the business and compatible with the pension provision.

- Do you know what discretionary powers there are and how these are exercised?
- Are there any unfunded pension promises outside of the designated pension schemes?
- Are you comfortable that the pension provision is compatible with other elements of employee benefit?
- Are you comfortable that any related insurances and protections are operating correctly?

## Your business structure

For a simple one company business with no pension scheme history, there should hopefully be no liabilities of the past to worry about. Your aim, therefore, is to get it right for the future.

It is important to get the operational structure clear and this starts at the top. Whether a one simple sentence or within a more extensive policy document, it should be possible to produce an unambiguous statement that says this is what we do on pensions. Regardless of business size, it would also be useful to identify a person on the board (or as an officer of the board eg company secretary) that has pensions responsibility on behalf the employer. It may not be an easy or obvious decision as most boards realistically would not be expected to include pensions experts. The importance here is to be clear of the reporting lines to avoid omission, duplication and time wasting. A pensions manager (if there is one) should logically then report to the person designated as the 'pensions director'. Smaller businesses would be hard pushed to justify a dedicated pensions manager making it more likely that the Director or Company Secretary designated with pensions responsibilities would need to be more active at the functional level in ensuring overall pensions management is effective.

Employers within larger groups will also need to be clear of reporting lines and authority levels upwards and within the group as a whole. It is also important to be perfectly clear on reporting lines for the chair of trustees.

Any pension practice locally should escalate downwards from the headline policy of the parent company. Whilst legally within the UK, there will be obligations on the UK-based companies, each operating company needs to know how much autonomy it has within the group.

- Who on behalf of the UK Board is regarded as pensions director in the UK?
- If the parent company is outside the UK, who is the point of contact at this higher level?
- Within the group, how many companies operate in the UK?
- Are UK subsidiaries empowered to make any local pensions decisions or expected to conform with policy decisions at a higher level?
- Is there a scheme that covers all UK companies within the group?
- For pension purposes, does a UK company have pension responsibilities beyond the UK? How does that work?
- Are there any partially owned businesses? Is pension responsibility clear?
- Are there businesses in the UK that do not operate within the same reporting structure for normal business purposes (eg different divisions). How do pensions fit in?

- Do any UK businesses have any pension responsibilities beyond the UK? How does that work?

Business reconstruction (sales/purchases/large scale redundancies) can be a risk if potential pension issues are not considered; care needs to be taken. Pensions can sometimes be a bit of an afterthought but can be critically important and needs thought as soon as possible in the process. Although defined contribution schemes are less of a worry than defined benefit, a shift of ownership (business or company) or change of employer is likely to have an impact of some sort. Defined benefit schemes are more of a headache and have been known to get in the way of an otherwise perfectly viable business sale. Whether buying, selling or restructuring internally, make sure you identify what pension schemes are relevant. These may not only be those that relate to the current employees. It may be possible to have transitional periods of ongoing membership in a current scheme but this is a potentially complex area that will require clear understanding of the options, consequences and the correct process to be followed including the decisions and processes that trustees may need to undertake.

# Know and manage your history

The process of producing company accounts should be a reasonably reliable way of identifying anything substantial but ultimately auditors can only assess what they've been given and should not be expected to know more than the company itself. What may be fairly immaterial for accounts purposes could be very significant to a long serving employee who may have been in several pension schemes during her or his working life with you. This person couldn't really care less about the distinction between trustees and employers. All he or she wants at retirement is clear information about all schemes where any benefits are held in order to make choices and be paid reliably. Some businesses have a very complex history with different company names, brand names, colloquial names and with legal company entities effectively swapping names, or perhaps a business sale where the limited company itself has stayed where it was. Whilst, legally, all companies should know without doubt where they have liability, there is arguably a moral aim also to be helpful to employees and ex-employees in identifying all schemes that may be relevant. This may in fact go beyond moral responsibility if there are doubts as to whether transfer values have or have not been made from one scheme to another. Some schemes for example may have provided an overall promise offsetting benefits from other predecessor schemes posing a risk of under or overpayment if the records are not joined up. Ultimately, there is also the question of data reliability. Data originates from the individual, to the employer, to the scheme administrator and then possibly transferred to another scheme or another administrator. Whilst each of these will be governed by data protection requirements, there is room for error on a number of occasions. It may well be impossible to remedy some historical problems but others may still be looming. As mentioned earlier, the termination of the ability to contract out of the state scheme in 2016 will force schemes to reconcile this element with the state records. As these relate back to what employers did on national insurance payments way back, this is an example of what could crawl out of the woodwork.

## Practical responsibilities and agents

The choice and design of a scheme is made by the employer. Make sure these decisions are made by the right group of people and recorded properly.

There may have been advisers up to this point on what to do, and part of setting up will be the formal registration of the scheme. However, to get it up and running, other parties will come into play and take us into the real world.

Make sure those at operational levels within your organization know what they are to do and who they are required to deal with. Regardless of the pension schemes chosen, company size pension strategy or trustee structure, the practical responsibilities at operational levels will make or break the success. The importance of this should not be underestimated at Board level. Beyond the strategy, there needs to be correct and consistent communication, efficient payroll and data processes and contribution payments etc.

When dealing with employees, there is likely to be a common sense approach that joining a scheme is the right thing to do for most people but there will be some exceptions, possibly at the higher level where limitations on tax allowances have an impact. In the practical world, your employees will come across many other aspects including divorce, parental leave, sickness, death, leavers, retirees, secondments, and agency workers. So, your employees need to know what to do and say and be helpful, and sensitive to circumstance BUT it is a risk if they give specific financial advice, and there is also a risk if there is not a full understanding of the composition of the workforce. For employer groups, the structure of the group and how the various employers interact in context of employment terms and decisions also need to be clear at these operational levels. There is big risk if data is unreliable.

There has been a lazy culture in pensions as a whole that over-uses the term 'trustees' ('trustees do this', 'trustees need to do that'). Trustees indeed have to make decisions and do things but it is rarely appropriate for members or administrators to be dealing with the trustees directly on a routine basis. There are many aspects involved (eg accounting, actuarial, legal, administration, investment etc.) and there can be a temptation to trespass into other camps. To avoid spiralling costs and to ensure proper control, it is very important to draw a distinction between functionality and advice.

Functionality is procedure-based. Regardless of whether an appointment is by the employer, the Trustees or jointly by both or as a sub-appointment by an agent, it needs to be very clear on what the job is, what the procedure is, who is doing what, and what the reporting lines are.

Individual advice is one thing and it needs to be clear how this will operate.

Advice beyond that should in the main be in the best interests of the whole but unfortunately can become a bit difficult if too much distinction is drawn between the interests of employers and the different interests of trustees. These do exist but should be managed by ensuring that any appointed agent is required to declare a conflict of interest, which can then be onwardly managed appropriate to the circumstance.

## Overall pensions management and co-ordination

There are major risks if there is uncertainty of facts or responsibility.

The employer has a responsibility to its employees to make sure pension provision is well managed.

Good governance at its simplest is knowing, and being able to demonstrate, that all aspects are efficient, thus managing risk and controlling liabilities.

Mike Redston, is co-owner of ARC Benefits Limited, a pensions management and governance specialist. Mike was formerly the pensions manager for a large multinational conglomerate for over 25 years, and has over 40 years' experience in the pensions industry. He is co-author of *108½ Tips to Tame Your Pensions Beastie*, a book on practical pensions management, and in his spare time is an orchestral conductor and writer of musicals.

# The legal background

## 2.2

*For HR or finance managers, Roderick Ramage gives a summary of how the law on pensions has evolved.*

'My Scottish Widows pension' is how an individual might describe her or his pension scheme, but, from a legal perspective, the main types of pension schemes are occupational and personal. They are defined in s1 of the Pension Schemes Act 1993, but a rule of thumb to identify them is to look for the following characteristics:

    **a** An occupational pension scheme is normally a tripartite relationship between (first) the employer, which establishes the scheme, appoints the trustees, pays contributions and is liable for any pension debt, (secondly) the trustees, who receive the contributions, invest them, administer the scheme and pay the benefits and (thirdly) members, who pay contributions and who and whose dependants receive benefits.

    **b** A personal pension scheme has, fundamentally, nothing to do with the employer. It is a bilateral contract between the member, who pays contributions and the provider, eg an insurance company, which pays the benefits. In the employment context this is commonly backed by a second bilateral contract between the employer, which pays contributions and provides a payroll deduction service and the employee. Even where the employer makes the arrangements and offers it to its employees, as in a grouped personal pension plan (or scheme), often called a GPPP, it is still a personal pension scheme.

## Trusts and trustees

Tax relief was originally made available for occupational pension schemes, then called superannuation funds, by the Finance Act 1921 on the condition that they were established under irrevocable trusts. The trust condition for favourable tax treatment ceased to apply when the Finance Act 2004 came into force on 'A-Day', 6 April 2006, but trusts have continued to be the normal legal structure of occupational pension schemes. The trust protects the pension funds from the employer and its creditors.

The employer usually has the power to appoint and remove the trustees, but the members have a right to nominate not less than one third of them or of the directors of a trustee company.

One commentator, when asked to weigh the merits of trust-based schemes against contract-based schemes (eg personal pension schemes), replied that the answer of the law is self-evident, because the sole duty of trustees is to pay money to the beneficiaries, while the sole duty of company directors and those whom they employ to work for the company, in this case the pension scheme provider, is to maximize the company's interests.

## Defined contributions or benefits

DC and DB are the abbreviations for defined contributions and defined benefits, the main differences between them are the fixed and variable factors.

In a DC scheme, commonly called money purchase, one knows the contributions, fixed amounts or percentages of pay, but not the pensions, which will depend on interest rates, investment returns, changes in longevity etc. over the member's working life and retirement. These schemes are therefore finance director friendly, because the cost is known, but they leave the whole risk of future changes in interest rates etc. on the members, who cannot know the amount of their pensions until they retire.

Conversely, in a DB scheme, the benefit is known in advance, commonly as a proportion of final or average salary (or, now rarely, specified amounts), but, for the same problem, ie future interest rates etc. are unknown, the cost of providing the benefits are not known and have to be estimated actuarially every three years. These schemes, if properly funded, are member friendly, as the employer, which typically pays the balance of the cost in excess of the member's fixed contributions, carries all the risk of future changes in interest rates etc.

Benefits in a hybrid scheme depend on which of two or more alternative methods of calculation produces the highest, or (in the statutory definition) lowest, rate or amount. For example, a scheme could give a money purchase benefit with a final (or average) salary underpin, or vice versa. The member's benefit in the first is the money purchase benefit, but if the underpin (commonly a guaranteed minimum pension) is higher, it is the higher that is paid, and conversely, if the scheme is DB but the contributions would have provided a higher DC benefit, the DC benefit will be given.

By the Pension Act 2015 the government has provided the legal framework for its proposals for new forms of pension provision to share the pension scheme risks as an alternative to the either/or types of schemes outlined above.

   i  Shared risks or defined ambition schemes: 'Defined Ambition' had been defined very widely and will include a partial guarantee of members' benefits. Interest, investment returns and longevity risks will therefore be shared between employers and employees.
   ii Collective defined contribution (CDC) schemes: Each member of a money purchase pension scheme, whether occupational or personal, has an individual fund all or part of which, will be converted into an annuity (unless it is all applied in drawdown). Therefore each member carries the risks of interest, investment returns and longevity. In a CDC scheme pensions will be paid out of the scheme's funds. The employer will not be required to 'top up' the fund, so the risks here are shared between the members.

These provisions and details for the new forms of pension will be brought into force by regulations at appointed dates, if and when the government proceeds with them.

## Death in service benefits

A typical final or average salary occupational pension scheme provides, on the death of a member in service, a lump sum of typically 4 times pay, but sometimes a lower and rarely a higher multiple and a pension for a surviving spouse or civil partner and, but not always, other dependants. The benefits are often but does not need to be insured. Occupational money purchase schemes can provide the same benefits, but some DB schemes provide no more than a lump sum equal to the value of the member's fund at the date of death.

If pensions are provided by a money purchase scheme, occupational or personal, it is common for the employer to provide at its expense a death in service benefit by a stand-alone insured death in service scheme, of which the employer is usually also the sole trustee. Typically these schemes provide only a lump sum benefit. Sometimes the employer puts all employees into the scheme, and not just those in the personal pension scheme, but usually the amount of the benefits is lower for employees who are not members of the money purchase scheme.

An unintended consequence of the statutory definition of an occupational pension scheme's activities (Pensions Act 2004 s255) is that stand-alone death in service schemes, despite having the tripartite relationship described in para 4(a) above, are not occupational, so the right to the benefit is not exempt transfer under TUPE (defined below).

# Transfer of Undertakings (Protection of Employment) Regulations 2006

The effect of the Transfer of Undertakings (Protection of Employment) Regulations 2006 (TUPE) on a transfer of an undertaking, in corporate finance terms usually called an assets sale, the employees in the undertaking and their contract terms are transferred automatically to the transferee or the buyer of the business. Regulation 10 exempts from transfer all benefits in an occupational pension scheme on old age and invalidity and for dependants. Personal pensions are not in this exemption and therefore pass under TUPE with the transferring employees' other rights. Other rights in occupational schemes, commonly known as Beckmann/Martin rights, typically rights to an unreduced pension on early retirement, usually in connection with redundancy, also pass under TUPE.

# Section 75 debt

Employers participating in DB schemes are also at risk for the pension debt under s75 of the Pension Act 1995 if the scheme is wound up or if there is an 'employment cessation event', ie if one employer in a multi-employer scheme ceases to employ at least one person as an active member of the scheme, while other employers continue to do so. The amount of the pension debt is the difference between the value of the scheme's assets and the amount required to secure the scheme's liabilities by the purchase of annuity and deferred annuity contracts. Even simple routine corporate restructuring and small sales can inadvertently cause an employment cessation event and trigger a s75 debt, unless one of the statutory withdrawal or apportionment arrangements are made.

# Accounting for pensions

Money purchase schemes are shown in company employer's accounts as the cost of the contribution. DB schemes are shown as capital values on a broadly similar basis to that used in their periodic actuarial valuations rather than as long term cash flows. For short articles about the s75 debt in multi-employer schemes and the treatment of pensions under FRS17 and IAS 19, see pension articles 38 and 32 at www.law-office.co.uk (accessed 25/10/15)

Roderick Ramage BSc (Econ) solicitor started his present sole practice in 1997 specializing in pensions law. His work is for trustees or employers and occasionally members in all aspects of pension and pension scheme law, particularly documentation, trustees' duties and compliance, corporate finance transactions, outsourcing and transfers of contracts, discrimination, members' rights, conflicts of interest, scheme merger, managing deficits and surpluses, closure and winding up. Often he works with other solicitors, whose clients' needs are affected by pensions, but the solicitors do not have their own pension law specialist. Because he has a long and deep experience of employment and general company and corporate finance work, his specialist pension law advice is firmly grounded in the wider aims and ethos of the parties involved.

Further details: Copehale Coppenhall Stafford ST18 9BW; 01785-223030 or 07785-707111; roderick.ramage@law-office.co.uk; www.law-office.co.uk

Authorized and regulated by the Solicitors' Regulation Authority number 231800

# Automatic enrolment

2.3

*By 2018, all employers will automatically be expected to enrol their employees into a pension scheme. Roderick Ramage explains what is legally required.*

Automatic enrolment (AE) applied first to employers of 120,000 or more, whose staging date (the date on which AE first applies to an employer) was 1 October 2012. Progressively smaller categories of employers have passed their staging date. Employers with fewer than 30 (as at 1 April 2012) in their PAYE scheme have their staging dates from 1 June 2015 to 1 April 2017 according to their PAYE reference numbers. The remainder, including new employers, have staging dates up to 1 February 2018, from when AE will apply to all employers. A new employer is one which first pays PAYE income between 1 April 2012 and (but not including) 1 October 2017. A pack for small and micro-employers is available at www.law-office.co.uk.

Every employer (there are no exceptions for small employers) must arrange for its jobholders to be enrolled automatically into an automatic enrolment scheme as an active member from the automatic enrolment date unless she or he is a member of a qualifying scheme.

A jobholder is an employee or a worker working in Great Britain under a contract, aged at least 16 and under 75 with qualifying earnings. The jobholders to be enrolled automatically are those who:

- are aged 22 and over and not over state pensionable age
- earn over £10,000 pa

Other jobholders may be enrolled voluntarily

A qualifying scheme is an occupational or personal pension scheme, which is registered under the Finance Act 2004 and meets the quality requirement:

If the scheme is a money purchase scheme, the minimum contribution to it are 8 per cent of qualifying earnings, which for 2015–16 are from £5,824 to £42,385 pa, of which, from October 2018, the employer must pay a minimum of 3 per cent, leaving the employee to pay 4 per cent and tax relief to provide the remaining 1 per cent.

Before October 2017 the rates are 1 per cent for each rising in October 2017 to 2 per cent for employers and 3 per cent for employees.

If the scheme is salary related, it must satisfy one of the following two tests:

- test scheme standard The scheme must provide a pension for life starting at age 65 or any higher age prescribed equal to 1/120th of average qualifying earnings (see (i) above) in the last three tax years before the end of pensionable service for each year of pensionable service up to 40 years. Alternatively it may provide a lump sum at that age to provide benefits.
- alternative test The cost of providing the benefits must not be less than the contributions necessary to satisfy the DC quality requirement

There are three alternatives to the 8 per cent contribution rate on qualifying earnings:

**i** 9 per cent of which the employer pays 4 per cent on the employees pensionable earnings if those earnings are equal to or exceed the jobholder's basic pay

**ii** 8 per cent of which the employer pays 3 per cent on the employees pensionable earnings if those earnings are equal to or exceed the jobholder's basic pay and, taking all the relevant jobholders together, their pensionable earnings are at least 85 per cent of their earnings

**iii** 7 per cent of which the employer pays 3 per cent on the jobholders total earnings

Jobholders have the right to opt out of their employers' AE schemes and have their contributions refunded. Jobholders, who opt out or give up membership of their employer's AE scheme or leave a qualifying scheme without joining the employer's AE scheme, must be re-enrolled on the employer's next automatic re-enrolment date, which, at the employer's choice, is not more than three months before nor three months after the third anniversary of its staging and each subsequent automatic re-enrolment date. Re-enrolment is immediate if the cessation results from an act or omission by the employer or a third party not at the jobholder's request.

There are provisions to protect jobholders and recruits from being pressured or encouraged to opt out, which if infringed can lead to a penalty not exceeding £50,000.

The penalties for breaches are fine, ranging from maxima of £50 a day where the employer has fewer than five jobholders to £10,000 a day where it has 500 or imprisonment not exceeding two years or both.

Roderick Ramage BSc (Econ) solicitor started his present sole practice in 1997 specializing in pensions law. His work is for trustees or employers and occasionally members in all aspects of pension and pension scheme law, particularly documentation, trustees' duties and compliance, corporate finance transactions, outsourcing and transfers of contracts, discrimination, members' rights, conflicts of interest, scheme merger, managing deficits and surpluses, closure and winding up. Often he works with other solicitors, whose clients' needs are affected by pensions, but the solicitors do not have their own pension law specialist. Because he has a long and deep experience of employment and general company and corporate finance work, his specialist pension law advice is firmly grounded in the wider aims and ethos of the parties involved.

Further details: Copehale Coppenhall Stafford ST18 9BW; 01785-223030 or 07785-707111; roderick.ramage@law-office.co.uk; www.law-office.co.uk

Authorized and regulated by the Solicitors' Regulation Authority number 231800

# Other legal duties

2.4

*Roderick Ramage summarizes what else an employer must do in providing pensions.*

## State pension

Everyone is entitled to the state basic pension, although the amount depends on each person's contribution record. All employees below state pension age and earning over the lower earnings limit (LEL) pays national insurance contributions up to the upper earning limit (UEL) respectively £112 pw and £815 pw for 2015–16. The employer too pays NICs but is not limited by the UEL.

The state basic and second pensions will be merged in a single flat rate pension from 6 April 2016, when contracting-out of the state second pension will cease. Employers and employees will both pay increased NIC because the NIC rebate will cease. The possible responses of employers with open contracted-out DB schemes are to:

  i  absorb the additional cost and keep the scheme as it is
  ii reduce scheme benefits
  iii increase members' contributions
  iv close the scheme

## Stakeholder pension schemes

The Pensions Act 2008, which introduced automatic enrolment, s87 abolished from 1 October 2012 an employer's obligation to provide a stakeholder pension scheme, but existing stakeholder schemes may continue, until and unless the employee withdraws his requests to the employer to deduct his contributions from his pay, and be used for automatic enrolment.

# TUPE and Pensions Act 2004

Under sections 257 and 258 of the Pensions Act 2004, employees transferring under TUPE, who are members of an occupational pension scheme or eligible for one or would be eligible on sufficient length of employment, are entitled to pension protection.

The TUPE article 10 exemption still applies, but an alternative scheme must be provided by the transferee. It can be DC or DB, but what is normal is to provide a stakeholder scheme, to which the employer matches the employee's contributions up to a maximum of 6 per cent of pay. In view of the abolition of the general stakeholder requirement it is curious that the government has retained the requirement for a stakeholder scheme in this context. In practice the provision of a GPPP with a charging structure matching that of a stakeholder scheme will probably be sufficient. If the transferor's obligation was to pay a rate below 6 per cent to a money purchase scheme (eg the lower rates payable under automatic enrolment), the 6 per cent maximum is reduced to the amount paid by the transferor: Transfer of Employment (Pension Protection) Regulations 2005 as altered with effect from 6 April 2014.

Employees with personal pension are treated differently (para 5 above) which can lead to an anomaly and an HR problem. If, of two employees being transferred under TUPE, one is in an occupational money purchase scheme and the other in a personal pension scheme, and in each case the employer's contributions are 10 per cent of pay and the employee 3 per cent :

- The employee in the occupational scheme will be entitled under s257 to contributions from the new employer of 3 per cent of pay and, even by increasing her or his contributions, cannot require the new employer to pay more than 6 per cent.
- In contrast, the employee in a personal scheme, which transfers under TUPE, remains entitled to contributions at the 10 per cent rate from the new employer while still paying only 3 per cent.

# Public sector outsourcing

Outsourcing is normally a transfer of an undertaking or a service to which TUPE applies. Public sector employees risked being transferred to a private sector contractor under TUPE and losing their valuable public sector final salary pension rights.

Fair Deal was intended to protect those rights. Fair Deal for Staff Pensions is guidance first issued by the Office of the Deputy Prime Minister in June 1999, under which public sector authorities should require contractors, to whom services are outsourced, to provide pensions for transferring employees pensions, which are the same as or broadly comparable with the transferring authority's public sector scheme. The 2014 guidance, for what is usually called New Fair Deal, states that the policy applies to transfers from central government and does not apply to transfers from local government and other best value authorities. The most significant change made by New Fair Deal is that, when it applies, the transferring employees will be entitled to stay in their public sector pension schemes, as a result of which the transferee will not be required to provide a scheme giving broadly comparable benefits. Guidance to New Fair Deal is available from the following link: https://www.gov.uk/government/publications/fair-deal-guidance (accessed 14/09/2015).

The 2007 Direction, which applies to only local and other best value authorities gives employees 'pension protection', ie a right to the pension rights to which they would have been entitled under their previous employment, which is normally done by permitting the transferring employees to remain in their present pension scheme.

## Industry-specific pensions

There are a number of instances in which an employer must provide membership of a particular scheme.

Membership of the Teachers' Pension Scheme is a right that a teacher has by virtue of her or his job, in some cases, automatically and in others either with election or with election and the employer's consent.

Privatization (eg the coal, electricity supply, railways, training boards) has given some employees, who were active members of the relevant industry pension scheme, the right to remain in the scheme or to join and remain in a scheme with comparable or no worse rights.

## Employment protection rights (pensions)

### Terms of employment

The statutory statement of terms of employment must contain or refer to a document, which contains particulars of pensions and pension schemes, and a statement whether a contracting-out certificate is in force (but see para 8(b) above).

### Compensation for unfair dismissal

Compensation for unfair dismissal can include the loss of pension rights. The compensation for the loss of money purchase rights is calculated by reference to the contributions, but the recommended calculation of the loss of final salary rights is complicated and assumes that the employer will never have access to another final salary scheme.

## Not to suffer detriment

Employees are not to suffer a detriment for being or performing acts as a trustee of an occupational pension scheme which relates to their employment.

## Paid time off

Employees are to have right to paid time off work for performing duties or training as a trustee of an occupational pension scheme which relates to their employment.

## Automatically unfair dismissal

The dismissal of an employee is automatically unfair if the reason or principal reason for the dismissal was that she or he performed or proposed to perform any functions as a trustee of an occupational pension scheme which relates to her or his employment or that any action was taken to enforce an employer's auto-enrolment obligation and the employer was prosecuted for its failure to comply.

> Roderick Ramage BSc (Econ) solicitor started his present sole practice in 1997 specializing in pensions law. His work is for trustees or employers and occasionally members in all aspects of pension and pension scheme law, particularly documentation, trustees' duties and compliance, corporate finance transactions, outsourcing and transfers of contracts, discrimination, members' rights, conflicts of interest, scheme merger, managing deficits and surpluses, closure and winding up. Often he works with other solicitors, whose clients' needs are affected by pensions, but the solicitors do not have their own pension law specialist. Because he has a long and deep experience of employment and general company and corporate finance work, his specialist pension law advice is firmly grounded in the wider aims and ethos of the parties involved.
>
> Further details: Copehale Coppenhall Stafford ST18 9BW; 01785-223030 or 07785-707111; roderick.ramage@law-office.co.uk; www.law-office.co.uk
>
> Authorized and regulated by the Solicitors' Regulation Authority number 231800

# Other legal options

2.5

*Roderick Ramage discusses what an employer may do above the legal minimum.*

The things that an employer must do are only a minimum. There is broadly speaking nothing to prevent the parties from agreeing whatever they wish as long as it is not less than the minimum. The only upper restrictions for a tax registered pension scheme are each member's annual and life time allowances for tax relief. Subject to these restriction and if the member is willing to suffer tax charges resulting from exceeding the allowances or to forego the tax advantages of a register scheme, an employer can be as generous as it wishes to be and can afford and give pensions in any way it wishes and agrees with its employees or any of them.

## No contractually compulsory membership

Employers cannot make membership of the employer's or any other pension scheme compulsory. Section 15 of the Social Security Act 1986 made void all terms to that effect and thereby started the pensions mis-selling scandal, in which employees were persuaded to leave their employers' occupational pension schemes, then largely final salary, and instead start personal pension schemes. Section 15 was repealed and replaced by s160 of the Pension Schemes Act 1993, which remains in force and is not be affected by AE. Employees enrolled automatically into a pension scheme who do not opt out during the opt out period, may cease to be active members of the scheme.

## Taxation

Schemes registered with HMRC under the Finance Act 2004 enjoy a degree of favourable tax treatment. The broad principles are:

a   tax relief is given on contribution, the scheme's income is tax free and benefits paid out of the scheme are taxed
b   there is no limit on the amount of benefits that can be provided, but amount of tax relief is governed by annual and lifetime allowances
c   the maximum amount to contributions that can be paid by or for a member is the whole of her or his taxable earnings up to the annual allowance, which for 2016–17 will remain £40,000 for most people
d   for those earning above £150,000 pa, the annual allowance will reduce by £1 for every £2 above £150,00, until it is £10,000 for those earning £210,000 and over
e   unused annual allowances from the three previous years may be carried forward to be set-off against any excess contributions in the current year
f   on every benefit crystallization event (BCE) the value of the benefit taken is tested against the member's lifetime allowance or the balance of it after previous BCEs
g   the common BCEs are:
   (i)    taking pension from a DB scheme
   (ii)   entering drawdown
   (iii)  buying a lifetime annuity
   (iv)   taking lump sums
   (v)    reaching age 75
   (vi)   death
   (vii)  transferring to qualifying recognized overseas pension schemes
h   penalties are charged on contributions in excess of the annual allowance, amounts in excess for the lifetime allowance and payments out of the scheme which are not authorized by the Finance Act 2004

# Employer-financed retirement benefits scheme (EFRBS)

One effect of the reduction of the annual allowance to £40,000 and the lifetime allowance to £1m is that registered pension schemes are becoming irrelevant to or play only a small part in retirement planning for the highly paid. The EFRBS is the modern equivalent of the pre-6 April 2006 funded unapproved retirement benefits scheme (FURBS) and, at the risk of over simplification typically differs from a registered pension scheme in the following features:

a   There are no annual or lifetime allowances
b   The income earned on the EFRBS' investments is not tax free
c   None of the Finance Act 2004 restrictions applies to either the kind of investments that can be made by an EFRBS or the payments out of it
d   No corporation tax relief is allowed to the employer and no income tax or NICs are charged on the employee when contributions are paid by the employer to an EFRBS
e   The member is liable to income tax and NICs on money drawn out of an EFRBS, and the employer then receives corporation tax relief to the extent of the member's drawings

## Pension flexibilities

In his spring 2014 budget speech the Chancellor announced the abolition of the legal requirement for annuitization and the ability of members of DB pension schemes to access their funds, which the Pension Act 2014 brought into effect from 6 April 2015. If the scheme rules of an occupational pension scheme or the terms of a contract-based pension scheme permit it, members have a right from age 55 to one or more of flexi-access draw-down, an uncrystallized funds pensions lump sum (UFPLS) and an annuity.

An employer with an occupational DC scheme is affected in three ways by these flexibilities:

a   Whether, in the case of an occupational scheme, to alter the scheme's rules to permit the flexibilities, and if so, how far? The initial tendency amongst schemes for the workforce is to allow the whole but not part of a member's fund to be applied to be applied as an UFPLS and not to allow flexi-access draw-down, so a member who seeks a greater degree of flexibility must transfer his fund to another scheme. A small scheme, however, particularly of the kind popularly called a SSAS, is likely to change its rules to permit every possible flexibility.
b   Ongoing contributions. The annual allowance of a member, who has accessed any of the flexible options, has a money purchase annual allowance limited to £10,000 pa including both employer's and employees' contribution. If the member is also an active member of a DB scheme the usual annual allowance of £40,000 remains available.
c   Automatic enrolment. The employer will be required to re-enrol on its next periodic automatic re-enrolment date a member, who takes the whole of her or his fund as an UFPLS, unless the member continues to contribute to a qualifying scheme.

Roderick Ramage BSc (Econ) solicitor started his present sole practice in 1997 specializing in pensions law. His work is for trustees or employers and occasionally members in all aspects of pension and pension scheme law, particularly documentation, trustees' duties and compliance, corporate finance transactions, outsourcing and transfers of contracts, discrimination, members' rights, conflicts of interest, scheme merger, managing deficits and surpluses, closure and winding up. Often he works with other solicitors, whose clients' needs are affected by pensions, but the solicitors do not have their own pension law specialist. Because he has a long and deep experience of employment and general company and corporate finance work, his specialist pension law advice is firmly grounded in the wider aims and ethos of the parties involved.

Further details: Copehale Coppenhall Stafford ST18 9BW; 01785-223030 or 07785-707111; roderick.ramage@law-office.co.uk; www.law-office.co.uk

Authorized and regulated by the Solicitors' Regulation Authority number 231800

# PART THREE
# Scheme choices

# Scheme creation for small employers

3.1

*Elmer Doonan at Dentons considers how to make pensions pay.*

Before the Government began its auto-enrolment implementation, setting up a new pension scheme was not usually part of a small employer's 'to do' list. Outside of the Government outsourcing arena with its 'Fair Deal' requirements, an employer's pension obligations in the UK were limited to designating a stakeholder scheme and sign posting it to its employees.

There are two basic reasons for a small employer to put in place a pension scheme:

- Legal compliance: there are minimum legal obligations that an employer must meet and if it does not there are legal sanctions.
- Employee recruitment and retention: pension contributions are (currently) tax privileged. A good quality pension can help with recruitment and retention of the talent an employer needs for its business.

## Legal requirements

Since October 2012 the Government has been phasing in auto-enrolment which will eventually require all UK employers to provide pensions for their employees. The obligation arises from an employer's staging date which is determined by the number of PAYE employees the employer had in its largest PAYE scheme as at 1 April 2012. Employers must auto-enrol UK qualifying workers into a pension scheme meeting minimum contribution standards, provide various notices and information to inform workers of their rights and keep the workforce under review (for example, an increase in wages may qualify a worker into the auto-enrolment requirements).

Every three years employers must reassess their workforce and enrol anyone who is not in a qualifying pension scheme.

The staging date system means that the largest UK employers were hit by these requirements first. This allowed the system to bed in before it applied to smaller employers. However, smaller employers have now either reached or are approaching their staging date. Failure to meet auto-enrolment obligations will result in fines and, in extreme cases, criminal liability.

So that is what you have to do. The next question is how you do it, and how to maximize the benefits you get from your pension scheme in recruitment and retention terms.

## Key issues for a small employer setting up a pension scheme

- Cost – set up and overheads
- Risk – how to minimize risk and avoid future risks
- Return – getting the benefit from your pensions expenditure

## Cost – bang for your buck

The two key types of scheme for smaller employers are master trusts (a pension trust for non-associated employers to pool administration costs), and group personal pensions.

As a general rule the more complex or bespoke a scheme, the more expensive it is likely to be to set up and run. What is best for your business will depend on whether legal compliance or retention and recruitment is more important to your business.

If you are looking for a pure 'compliance' approach there is NEST. This is a master trust set up by the Government to provide a 'safe harbour' for employers who want to meet their auto-enrolment obligations. It has a duty to accept any employer needing an auto-enrolment solution and offers a basic compliance solution. Both costs and functionality are relatively limited.

Other, more complex master trusts include the People's pension and NOW pensions. All have websites and are able to provide information on joining costs and options available to members.

Contract-based group personal pensions are provided by insurers and consist of an agreement between the employer and provider on some basic administrative and cost issues, and personal pension products provided to employees directly by the provider. Most (and some master trusts) will have minimum volume requirements as a pension product can be uneconomical if it only serves half-a-dozen employees paying in minimum contribution rates.

It is possible for an employer to set up its own trust-based scheme. In practice this is not normally advisable as it is expensive, complex to administer and the Pensions Regulator has said it does not believe this sort of scheme has the resources to be a good quality pension scheme in the current market.

All of these options take time to implement so it is vital to prepare a good project plan for meeting your auto-enrolment obligations as many providers are going to be swamped with last minute applications from small employers who are looking to put in place a sticking plaster scheme to meet their legal obligations.

You will also need to put HR systems in place to deduct contributions and pay them to your provider. Some providers may offer this option but with others you may be expected to provide your own middle ware solution. HMRC's PAYE software offers some limited pension functionality and there are a variety of paid offerings. You will need to factor this into your considerations.

# Risk – meeting current obligations and protecting against future ones

When people think of risk and pensions they tend to think of defined benefit pension schemes. In today's pension environment it would be bordering on insanity to use such a pension structure (save where required due to public sector outsourcing rules) and so you need to consider the risks associated with defined contribution pension schemes.

- Legal risks – you need to comply with the auto-enrolment and anti-discrimination legislation
- Future legislative change – pensions in the UK are in a state of flux. Minimum auto-enrolment contributions will increase in 2017 and 2018. They may well increase further. The tax system for pensions is currently under review. The only real protection here is to keep up to date on requirements and your provider should be able to assist with this.
- Future litigation risks: You choose what pension scheme to provide to your employees. This creates the risk they will look to you if that scheme has high management charges or has poor investment returns. You will need to regularly benchmark your scheme against the market.

In order to mitigate the third head small employers will need to keep their pension scheme under review to make sure it is market competitive. Key areas include investment options: in particular the default fund since your employees money will be parked here if they do not make an alternative investment choice and have high management charges which can have a big impact on a member's pension outcome.

Key sources of information for employers include trustee reports for master trusts and the annual Independent Governance Committee reports for contract-based schemes. Master trusts may also have adopted the ICAEW assurance framework for master trusts which has received the backing of the Pensions Regulator.

## Return – retaining/recruiting employees

Your money is going into your employees' pensions. How can you make them value this?

Communication is key. Be clear what you are offering and how your employees benefit from the pension. Providers can often help with this. Obviously, there is a happy medium here between good communication and making promises that could rebound on you, but the auto-enrolment standard communications from the Pensions Regulator are a good start.

For higher earners more bespoke arrangements may be appropriate. SIPPs (self-invested personal pensions) provide a broader range of investment options and can be used for business related purposes. They cannot be used for auto-enrolment but can be a useful additional tool to retain staff.

> Elmer Doonan is a Partner and head of pensions in Dentons' London office. Dentons is the world's largest law firm providing tailored solutions to meet the local, national and global needs of clients in 125 locations in over 50 countries. Telephone 02072467151 E-mail: elmer.doonan@dentons.com; www.dentons.com

# The pensions landscape

3.2

*Dean Wetton reviews which schemes and what actions might now lead to the best outcomes for employees.*

Auto-enrolment, where every employer has to enrol all qualifying employees into a pension scheme, is well under way. We believe that most employers want their employees to get the most out of their pensions. While the primary determinant of outcomes is how much you and your employer contribute, there are other ways to improve likely outcomes for pension scheme members. We have conducted some research for the Defined Contribution Investment Forum on active governance in Defined Contribution (DC) pension funds. Once you have identified the scheme fiduciaries or whoever is responsible for the scheme, which can be a challenge in itself on DC contracts, six easily actionable changes can be pursued to improve outcomes for members:

- Set goals
- Have active asset allocation
- Review and monitor performance
- Ensure members get value for money
- Communicate the important issue – increase contributions
- Improve the at-retirement process

Many human resource managers feel that they have taken care of their pension responsibilities by putting a group personal pension from an insurer in place. However, when asked whether they had reviewed this recently or asked whether the offering was still up to scratch they are, at best, hesitant. they prefer to answer by saying that their firm already had trustees on their defined benefit or final salary scheme and had no further appetite for taking on pension trusteeships for defined contribution pensions too, but they now clearly saw the gap. This is something that we considered some years ago when setting up our business and tried to consider what the future might hold for pensions. We came up with a framework looking at effort put in by employers vs likely outcome for members (see figure on next page).

## Scheme Choices

**Quality** (vertical axis: Low to High) vs **Cost or effort to employer** (horizontal axis: Low to High)

Scheme positions on chart:
- MT (Master Trust): High quality, low-mid cost
- NEST: High quality, mid cost
- Stakeholder: Low-mid quality, low cost
- GPP (Group Personal Pension): Low-mid quality, low-mid cost
- SIPP: Mid quality, mid cost
- GPP (+ Gov Com): Mid quality, mid-high cost
- Own Trust: High quality, high cost

**Key**

**MT** Master Trust
**SIPP** Self-Invested Personal Pension
**GPP** Group Personal Pension
**Gov Com** Governance Committee

● Regulated by tPR     ● Regulated by FSA

---

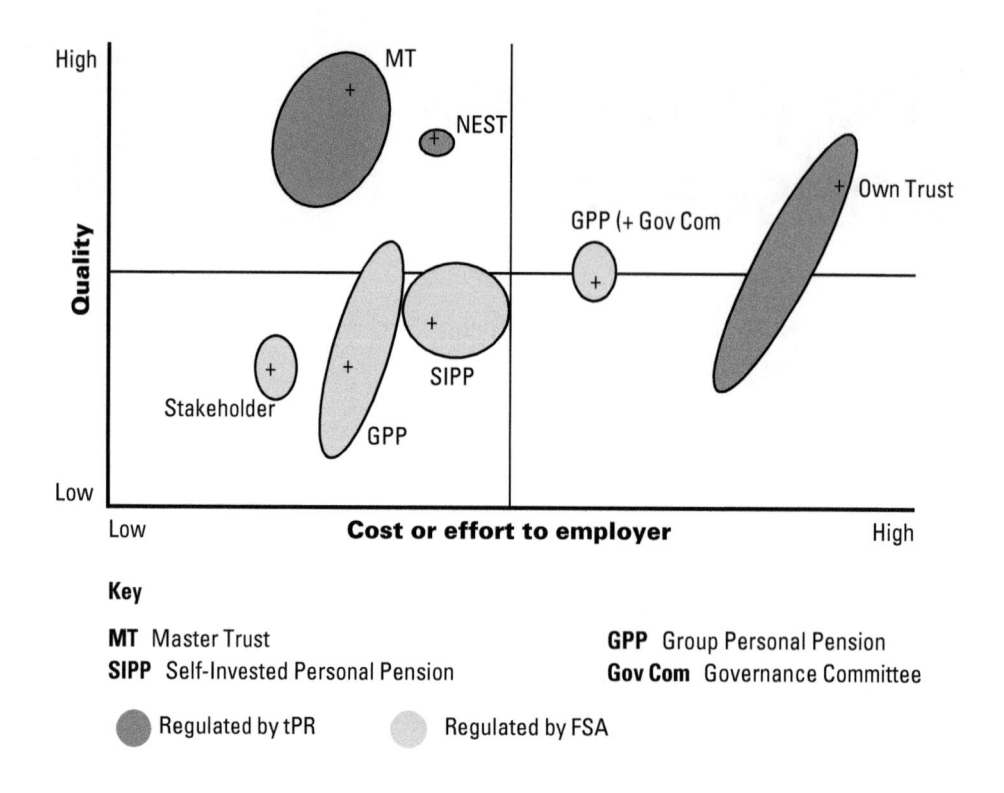

To give some reference points, we thought about the quickest, easiest scheme for employers to put in place: stakeholder personal pensions. Now we have reviewed a few of these over the years and while they may have looked cheap they seldom seemed to represent good value. A bit like the cheap toy that falls apart after a few days. At the other end of the scale is the employers own trust. This is like a DIY job at home – if you are skilled and put a lot of effort into it you get a pretty good job, but if you don't have much time and don't really know what you are doing the outcome is poor but it has still taken quite a lot of effort.

GPPs and SIPPs fall somewhere between own trust and stakeholder. Even with a governance committee, a GPP is limited as the committee can't easily implement the six changes; it is up to the insurer whether this is done or not.

## Trust vs contract: different regulators

All the red types of pension scheme are contract-based, that is each member has a contract with an insurer. By far the most common of these is the group personal pension usually arranged by independent financial advisers or employee benefit consultants and historically often sold on a commission basis.

Only the trust-based environment puts the scheme fiduciaries in a position to do this. In fact, this is an obligation to act on the members' best interests. They work in different circumstances and under different regulators. Trust-based fall under The Pensions Regulator while insurer-based contracts fall under the Financial Conduct Authority.

Of the things that the Financial Conduct Authority has to do, the ongoing monitoring of pensions is not the highest priority; they tend to be more concerned with how pensions are sold. This is why the previous pensions minister introduced Independent Governance Committees to have oversight over insurance-based workplace pensions. They are due to publish their first reports on 'value for money' in April 2016. This should make interesting reading.

Organizations are typically wary of the commitment involved in setting up their own trust-based pension arrangements, many still reeling under the legacy of their final salary commitments. But not all trusts have to be set up by a single employer.

That brings us on to Mastertrust. This is not a new thing. Some have existed for years. What is new is that the DC only focus and new entrants coming in. The Department of Work and Pensions looked at this and reached the same conclusion when developing the government sponsored scheme, the National Employment Savings Trust; it has to be trust-based. Mastertrusts offer the members this trustee protection but without the responsibility falling on the employer and the best mastertrusts are looking at these changes to improve outcomes for their members. This is why the Pensions Policy Institute is predicting some 50 per cent of all pension savers will be in a mastertrust by 2020.

Dean Wetton Advisory Limited is a boutique pensions and investment advisory firm founded in 2009 with some £15bn assets under advice and a global client base. Dean Wetton Advisory Limited is an appointed representative of Red Sky Capital LLP which is authorized and regulated by the FCA. For further information, please visit www.deanwettonadvisory.com

# The International Solution

**Multinational employers with mobile employees require a global solution**

In an increasingly global economy companies are now facing some of the pensions issues that once affected only the very largest employers. There are many fast growing multinational employers with mobile employees or operations in lesser developed countries.

An international pension or savings plan, based in a highly respected financial cent[re] allows the employer, whether large or small, to bring together all current and futur[e] pension provision in one structured arrangement.

With over 35 years' experience in the provision of international pension arrangeme[nts] the BWCI Group in Guernsey is well placed to solve the issues facing an increasing number of multi-national companies seeking to attract and retain the talent in the new global workforce.

**The solutions are here and available now.**

If you'd like to know more call Mike Freer on +44 (0) 1481 728432 or visit www.bwcigroup.com

A member of Abelica Global

# International pension plans

## 3.3

*How can pension promises to internationally mobile workers best be fulfilled, asks Carl Hansen, international director at BWCI.*

There is an increasing interest in international pension plans due to the trend towards globalization of businesses and the increasing challenges of retaining globally mobile employees in domestic pension plans. They are typically established in international finance centres such as the Channel Islands, the Isle of Man or Bermuda in order to benefit from flexible fiscal and regulatory regimes. International pension plans can pose unusual challenges to human resources directors in balancing conflicting demands. On the one hand, they may have an objective of parity with domestic employees while taking into account the differing fiscal and social insurance arrangements at home and overseas. On the other hand, flexibility and proportionality may be more important drivers where relatively small numbers of globally mobile employees are involved.

An international (or offshore) pension plan may be described as a pension or savings plan established in an international finance centre (the home country of neither the employer nor the employees) to provide benefits typically for the internationally mobile staff of a multinational group. For example, a UK multinational company might establish an international pension plan in Guernsey to provide retirement benefits for its international staff working in Africa or Asia. The plan can sometimes also be used to encompass locally recruited staff in overseas locations where it is more efficient to arrange their pension provision through a global pension plan because of the lack of local pensions and savings vehicles or to take advantage of economies of scale.

International staff might be career expatriates, or may be temporary or permanent transfers from one country to another within a multinational's group of companies. This group may also be referred to as mobile employees or third country nationals (TCNs).

Many international pension plans are established because the alternatives have been considered and found unsuitable. It is not generally practical for a multinational group to retain all its global employees in a home country pension plan. Some countries may allow mobile employees to remain in a home country plan for only a limited time.

Equally, the pension arrangements (if any) of the local overseas subsidiary company are unlikely to be suitable for international staff posted there for a limited period. Such local arrangements are designed in the local currency to meet the needs of the local staff, having regard to the available local social security benefits, local expectations and the local cost of living, and may well not meet the requirements of any international staff working in that location. In particular, international staff may not work in any location long enough to build up a full social security contribution record, and may not qualify under any local vesting requirements for occupational benefits either. Moreover, few international staff retire in the country of their assignment and those career expatriates with a series of overseas postings would not wish to accumulate a number of small deferred benefits denominated in a variety of currencies en route (if the vesting conditions are satisfied). International staff are unlikely to appreciate retirement benefits denominated in the currencies of certain emerging economies and overseas transfer payments may not be available

In recent years, there has been some limited development of pan-European pension plans. In theory, a pan-European plan can provide a single pension plan for all of an employer's European employees. However, the legal, taxation, and social insurance difficulties have made them costly for all but larger employers to operate. Also, current solvency requirements leave little flexibility for funding. Even if pan-European plans continue to develop, they will not provide a complete solution for most multinational groups, as their activities will extend beyond the EU boundaries. International pension plans and pan-European plans can complement each other in a well designed benefits programme.

An additional reason for establishing or extending the scope of an international pension plan can be to provide benefits for local staff where there are no suitable local investment vehicles for pension provision, or in order to gain from greater economies of scale when investing the assets. These workers may be excluded from participating in local retirement plans due to their expatriate status, or they could be local workers with limited options for retirement provision. Typical employers are large international oil or mineral extraction operations, as some countries rich in mineral or other natural resources may not have a well-developed pension structure.

In an increasingly global economy, smaller multinationals are now facing some of the benefits issues once only affecting the very largest employers. There are many fast growing companies with only informal or less uniform pension promises in place for internationally mobile workers. This often takes the form of a verbal or written promise that the mobile employee will be no worse off than if they had stayed in the home country benefit plans. Such promises are often not clear (especially when they must be interpreted a number of years later at retirement by those unfamiliar with the original situation) and it may be uncertain which group operating company should be meeting the cost of the promise made many years previously. They can also vary by individual, and they may lead to unintended inconsistent treatment of similarly situated employees. An international pension plan allows the employer to bring together all current and future promises in one structured arrangement. This also makes it much easier for various company departments to share information and to collaborate on funding, accounting, or risk benefit issues.

The inherent flexibility of international pension plans allows then to function more as savings vehicles than as traditional pension plans. International staff can accumulate funds in a central repository denominated in a widely traded currency. The plan can often be designed so that benefits can be paid at a time and in a form that best fit the individual circumstances of each member.

Carl Hansen is International Director at the BWCI Group in Guernsey in the Channel Islands. He qualified as a Fellow of the Society of Actuaries (US) in 1996 and earned a Diploma in International Employee Benefits in 2001. He specializes in international actuarial and other consultancy services to multinational employers. During his career, Carl has had in depth experience with retirement plans and other benefits issues in the US and many other jurisdictions around the world, including establishing and implementing international pension plans.

# PART FOUR
# Legacy and recovery

# Pension restructuring

4.1

*To repair deficits within final salary schemes, Elmer Doonan at Dentons discusses the options for mitigating liabilities.*

According to the Pension Protection Fund's (PPF) Purple Book 2015 there are just under 6,000 defined benefit (DB) pension schemes in the UK. Most are in deficit on the technical provisions basis under Part 3 of the Pensions Act 2004 and virtually all are in deficit on a buy-out basis under section 75 of the Pensions Act 1995. For many employers deficit repair contributions are a significant financial strain and meeting the buy-out deficit would result in bankruptcy. Seeking to avoid these liabilities would inevitably lead to the Pensions Regulator imposing a contribution notice or a financial support direction on the employer or companies connected or associated with the employer requiring it or them to meet them. Whilst it is ill-advised for an employer to seek to avoid all liability for its pension deficit there are steps that can be taken to restructure a DB pension scheme in order to mitigate that liability so that the deficit does not continue to grow and, in time, decreases.

Before any proposed restructuring of a DB pension scheme is undertaken the powers in the governing Trust Deed and Rules must be checked to see what is possible as the documentation and history of all DB schemes differ. Contracts of employment and announcements to members should also be checked. Once this has been done and decisions made on the restructuring that should take place it may be necessary to carry out a statutory consultation with members and employees on the proposed changes.

The nature of any restructuring and how radical it is will depend on what previous steps have already been taken to restructure the scheme. The possible options that might be adopted are set out below. Several of these options might be adopted at the same time depending upon how radical a restructuring is necessary.

# 1. Scheme open to new members and future pension accruals

The PPF's Purple Book 2015 indicates that 13 per cent of DB schemes remain open to new members/future accruals. These schemes provide the greatest cope for restructuring. One or more of the following options may be available:

    a  Closure of scheme to new members: PPF's Purple Book 2015 indicates that 51 per cent of DB schemes are now closed to new members. For those that remain open this would be a first step in controlling DB pension costs. It would involve a statutory consultation and consideration of an alternative, probably a defined contribution (DC), pension arrangement which meets auto-enrolment requirements for new employees.

    b  Closure to future accruals: PPF's Purple Book 2015 states that 34 per cent of DB schemes are closed to future accruals. This would be a major step in stemming DB pension liabilities and cutting future funding costs. A statutory consultation would be necessary and an alternative DC arrangement which meets auto-enrolment requirements would have to be considered for existing members. Contracts of employment should be reviewed to see if any employees have a contractual right to pension under the existing DB scheme.

    c  Reduce accrual rate: This is an alternative to closure to future accruals aimed at reducing future funding costs. Typically, 1/60ths and higher accrual rates could be reduced for future pensionable service. Accruals rates cannot be changed retrospectively as this would breach section 67 of the Pensions Act 1995. A statutory consultation would be necessary and consideration should be given to whether changing now to a DC arrangement might be more appropriate in the long term.

    d  Restrict pensionable pay: Pension costs could be reduced by restricting the amount of an employee's remuneration that is treated as pensionable in the future. This could be restricted to basic pay where, currently, it includes matters such as bonuses and overtime or capped at a specified level or could exclude or limit the amount of future pay increases that are pensionable. It is possible to achieve such changes under contractual arrangements between the employer and the members where this is not feasible by amending the scheme rules.

    e  Increase member contributions: If future DB pension accruals are to continue members could also be required to pay increased contributions. The affordability of the increases for the members should be considered as they could result in members leaving the scheme or trigger demands for pay increases to cover the cost to them. There would also need to be statutory consultation on this change.

**f** Increase normal retirement age: Many schemes increased the normal retirement age for women from 60 to 65 following the Barber judgment on the equalising normal retirement ages for men and women in 1990. At present, increases in the state pension age are being phased in. If normal retirement age is below age 65 this could be increased to 65. If it is age 65 it might be increased to 67 or more. Any such changes would apply only in respect of future service so the immediate effect on funding may be limited.

**g** Review early retirement rules: Generous early retirement rules can add significant funding costs and consideration ought to be given to changing them. For example, members with 10 years' service may be able to retire after age 60 without a reduction for early payment or members who retire early in grounds of ill-health may have prospective service to normal retirement date taken into account in calculating their pension.

## 2. Scheme closed to future accruals

**a** If a DB scheme is closed to future accruals there are options for seeking to further limit liabilities and deficit repair contributions:

**b** Reduce rate of annual pension increases and revaluation of deferred pensions: DB pension schemes are required to provide statutory annual pension increases. For pension accrued before 6 April 2005 the increase or revaluation must be inflation up to a maximum of 5 per cent and for pension accrued after that date inflation up to 2.5 per cent . Originally, inflation was measured by reference to LPI but is now measured by reference to CPI. Significant savings on funding costs can be achieved by changing to CPI but whether this is possible will depend on the wording of the pension increase rule.

**c** Pension increase exchange (PIE): Many pension schemes provide pension increases in excess of the statutory minimum. Since annual pension increase costs can significantly increase DB liabilities one way to deal with this is through a PIE. A PIE offers members the chance to exchange future non-statutory increases for a larger non-increasing pension and this can be attractive to many members depending on their circumstances. From an employer perspective a PIE can reduce the deficit and lead to lower deficit repair contributions.

**d** Enhanced transfer amounts: Reducing scheme membership can reduce deficit and funding costs through offering members who have left the company enhanced transfer values out of the scheme. The company would need to fund the costs of the enhanced transfers and ensure that the exercise was carried out in line with Pensions Regulator guidance on such exercises. There would be an initial cost involved that ought to be recouped if the exercise is successful.

e  Final salary link exchange: The rules of many DB schemes provide that even if closed to future accrual, the pension is to be based on salary at date of leaving or retirement. If salary increases are significant then it may be appropriate to enter a final salary link exchange so that members receive an enhanced pension in return or giving up this link.

Elmer Doonan is a Partner and head of pensions in Dentons' London office. Dentons is the world's largest law firm providing tailored solutions to meet the local, national and global needs of clients in 125 locations in over 50 countries. Telephone 02072467151 E-mail: elmer.doonan@dentons.com; www.dentons.com

# Rothesay life

▪ Secure, long-term pension de-risking.

▪ Tailor-made solutions.

▪ Leading UK life insurance company.

Rothesay Life was established in 2007 and has grown to be a leading UK life insurer:

**Over 213,000** pension fund members insured

**Over 160** transactions with pension funds

**£701 million** paid to policyholders in 2014

**£14.1 billion** of assets under management

**Over £3.5 billion** invested in UK projects, including in transportation, infrastructure, housing and utilities

Rothesay Life is proud to support
ageUK

www.rothesaylife.com
Tel: +44 (0)20 7770 5300

# Legacy options

4.2

*Doing nothing is not an option. Guy Freeman at Rothesay Life considers the different ways in which pension deficits can be managed.*

You could be forgiven for thinking that running a business these days requires you to be something of an expert in the field of occupational pensions.

Your final salary scheme may no longer be accepting new entrants – or even contributions to build up future benefits – but while it remains, it saps cash and resources and worse still, poses a potential threat to the business itself.

## It's a wind-up

As a result of pension legislation changes over the last 20 years, designed to protect employees and prevent another Robert Maxwell scandal happening, employers cannot simply walk away from their final salary schemes.

The governance requirements are onerous and the costs and burden of funding these schemes mean many companies do not want to deal with them any longer.

But they are caught in a cleft stick, as employers must secure the full value of the benefits when they wind their scheme up, typically through a bulk annuity buyout policy with an insurance company.

The insurance premium almost always exceeds the assets in the fund, and your options will depend on the size of the gap and how much time you have to bridge it. The focus of this article is on the more difficult but increasingly common situation for directors where the gap is too big to bridge.

## The options

If buyout is not affordable now, you might consider asking the pension fund trustees to take risk in their investment strategy and hope that the position improves over time. The aim will be to generate an extra return on the pension fund assets and to reduce the amount of extra capital injection required to be able to afford the buyout. This can work where there is time to bridge the gap and the necessary amount of investment risk is not excessive.

The Pensions Regulator is increasingly focused on the strength of employer covenants. If you're not strong enough to tolerate the risk in the investment strategy, you can forget it, as the regulator won't entertain the idea.

Any gains or losses from the scheme's investments will impact on the business and its value. So your board will also need to be happy that it is right for the shareholders to bear this investment risk as part of their investment in the business.

Once the investment approach is agreed then the next step is to agree how much additional cash to put in the pension fund each year. The government has allowed companies some leeway to retain cash in order to grow the business instead of forcing them to fund their pension deficits. However you will still need to demonstrate to the trustees that the members are suitably protected from loss of benefits through a combination of the strength of the business coupled with the proposed funding package.

## A clean break

Where the pension fund is a significant burden on the company it is often not possible to find a solution that works for the shareholders and the trustees. In these cases the future of the business is in jeopardy. An option in these circumstances is to separate the company from the scheme. This can be done by agreeing with the trustees a final payment that amounts to a compromise on the potential debt to the pension fund.

This payment would not be the full debt on wind-up, but would secure an acceptable proportion of the benefits. This will mean that the members do not receive their full benefits but this could be the best deal for the members if they end up with more than they would on insolvency. If released from this debt, the company may be able to continue to operate and even raise finance to fund the cost of this payment without the scheme's liabilities hanging over it. This can often create additional value that can be shared between the shareholders and the pension fund members not least because insolvency is avoided but also because the business may be able to grow again.

There are precedents for this. In 2011, the Uniq pension fund ceded 90 per cent of its shareholder's equity to the pension scheme making the scheme the largest shareholder. Freed of the burden of the £430m deficit, a buyer was quickly found and the company purchased for £113m. The scheme then used this capital along with the scheme's assets to enter into a pension buyout agreement.

More recently, MIRA (the Motor Industry Research Association) completed a compromise with its trustees as part of a new investment by HORIBA to acquire and develop the business.

## A hard sell

This will only work if the Pensions Regulator is convinced that if such a deal is not reached, then insolvency is inevitable.

Insolvency has generally been assessed on a 'going concern' basis over a 12-month horizon, but the Financial Reporting Council's (FRC) amended code of conduct is beginning to change views about what insolvency means (see box).

The code considers the appropriate timeframe for assessing viability as now being more than 12 months and this may influence the Pensions Regulator to look beyond its current 12-month stance towards a longer term horizon of three or five years as well.

Longer periods will catch the next scheme valuation, which may show the funding strain is expected to have worsened considerably, making the pension fund a far greater issue for the company and its future viability.

The alternative is to do nothing and carry on regardless. If the scheme drags the company down, the members will only have the protection of the Pension Protection Fund (PPF) – a safety net to which nearly every final salary scheme pays a levy.

That will be cold comfort to other stakeholders – shareholders – who will get nothing and may prefer to make a deal with the trustees which at best could leave them with a remnant of the old company from which they can rebuild and potentially provide benefits for the members in excess of PPF compensation.

## What next?

Doing nothing is really not an option in the current environment.

If you have a DB plan, it is almost certainly in deficit. Moreover investment markets since 2008 and the impact of quantitative easing have not been kind to funding positions. If you have time to repair the situation then market movements may be helpful if you are lucky.

If there isn't the time or the ability to repair the deficit then insolvency need not be the outcome.

If nothing else, develop an exit plan with the trustees to prepare for insurance. Check that the benefits are correct and clean up your scheme's data. Poor information adds costs and delays and can result in an extra premium if and when you get to the point of entering into a deal with an insurer.

Final salary schemes are not going to disappear just because they are ignored. Only positive, direct action, even if the scope is limited, will help to protect the business from the burden of these legacy schemes.

### The FRC governance code

The Financial Reporting Council's UK Corporate Governance Code provides guidance to UK listed businesses on best practice in this field.

Section C covers the responsibility of boards to determine the risks facing the business and report what it has done to meet them through its risk management and internal controls.

However, a new clause was added in October 2014 that introduced guidance on long-term viability statements.

It says that, having taken account of the current position, directors should explain in the annual report 'how they have assessed the prospects of the company, over what period they have done so and why they consider that period to be appropriate.

'The directors should state whether they have a reasonable expectation that the company will be able to continue in operation and meet its liabilities as they fall due over the period of their assessment, drawing attention to any qualifications or assumptions as necessary.' (For more see http://bit.ly/FRCcode2014)

It is important to note this guidance is for listed companies and is voluntary. The Code operates on a 'comply or explain' basis and it is for shareholders to enforce it, but this timeframe of long-term viability is likely, in time, to be adopted by other agencies such as the Pensions Regulator.

---

Guy Freeman is Co-Head of Business Development at Rothesay Life, one of the leading providers of regulated insurance solutions in the UK market for pensions de-risking, making payments of around £700m a year from over £19 billion of insurance contracts. In 2015, Rothesay Life received over £2.5 billion of bulk annuity premiums from pension funds to date (2014: £1.7bn). This strong growth has been achieved through the steady accumulation of pension scheme clients and significant strategic acquisitions.

Existing Rothesay Life clients include the pension schemes and members associated with such names as RSA, British Airways, Lehman Brothers, Rank, Uniq, General Motors, the MNOPF (Merchant Navy Officers Pension Fund), InterContinental Hotels, Philips, GKN and the Civil Aviation Authority.

Telephone: +44 (0)20 7770 5300 E-mail: Guy.Freeman@Rothesaylife.com
www.rothesaylife.com

**Picture this: A new way to offer retirement choices.**

Picture this: A brand new way to offer access to affordable expert help with retirement decisions. Our groundbreaking digital tools and advice services help workplace pension scheme members achieve the right retirement outcomes.

For the full picture, get in touch today.

email **Corporate.Solutions@lv.com**
or call **08000 850 260**

**LV=**
**Corporate Solutions**

---

Liverpool Victoria Friendly Society Limited: County Gates, Bournemouth BH1 2NF. LV= and Liverpool Victoria are registered trademarks of Liverpool Victoria Friendly Society Limited (LVFS) and LV= and LV= Liverpool Victoria are trading styles of the Liverpool Victoria group of companies. LVFS is authorised by the Prudential Regulation Authority and regulated by the Financial Conduct Authority and the Prudential Regulation Authority, register number 110035. Liverpool Victoria Financial Advice Services Limited (LVFAS), registered in England No. 3027145, is authorised and regulated by the Financial Conduct Authority, register number 186890. LVFAS is a wholly owned subsidiary of LVFS. Registered address for both companies: County Gates, Bournemouth BH1 2NF. Telephone: 01202 292333. **2254-2015 10/15**

# DB transfers

## 4.3

*Steve Lewis at LV= Corporate Solutions discusses how to create a fair and robust process for DB transfers.*

This section considers how trustees and employers can assist members to make informed choices and ensure good retirement outcomes. The 'de-risking' opportunities for scheme sponsors and the attractions for scheme members means that a DB transfer has the potential to create a win-win situation which is fair and responsible whilst protecting the interests of both the sponsor and member.

Combined with effective member communications to secure their engagement, these simple steps can help employers and trustees to provide a substantial benefit to both parties:

### 1. Provide easy-to-understand information and modelling tools to allow members to understand the risks

Behavioural economists have shown how people exhibit a considerable overconfidence bias. In the world of DB transfers this overconfidence manifests itself in four key components:

- over-estimate of the investment returns over time
- under-estimate the volatility of the returns
- under-estimate how long they will live
- under-estimate their essential income and the effects of inflation

Customer-facing tools to educate customers on inflation, investment and budgeting tools are available although there has been limited progress on longevity modelling. LV= has developed a new interactive tool – *LV= Pension Compass* – which is designed to help members of DB schemes understand the implications of a DB transfer and to make informed decisions. This includes providing longevity data down to postcode level to allow members to model the probability of them running out of funds. It also offers the option of advice from a professional financial adviser.

LV= Pension Compass complements LV='s fully regulated online retirement advice tool – 'LV= Retirement Wizard'. This ground-breaking tool is best-suited to

DC schemes and is designed to offer access to information and advice for members at a competitive cost and at a time and pace to suit them.

## 2. Review the scheme terms and conditions to allow partial transfer of benefits

A transfer from DB to DC is a large shift of risk to the member. The ability to allow partial transfers would help to mitigate this movement in risk and provide more flexibility. Unfortunately many schemes do not allow this at present. Key reasons behind this are the increased administrative burdens in maintaining records and calculating the partial transfer, especially when the member may have more than one shape of benefits with different transfer values. A partial transfer will enable greater flexibility for the next step.

## 3. Partner with an advisory firm that has a minimum income requirement advisory principle

The minimum income requirement disappeared from April 2015, however it is well established that the minimum income for retired people in the UK to enjoy a comfortable retirement is in excess of the state pension. The Joseph Rowntree foundation publishes a minimum income standard every year for different demographic groups. Their 2014 report showed that the minimum retirement income requirement was approximately £15k a year. To mitigate longevity and inflation risk from the DB transfer process, all advisory firms should look to secure an essential income amount, either via a partial transfer or the purchase of an annuity. Many advisory firms have abandoned the minimum income requirement, but for DB transfers this principle remains a cornerstone of providing good member outcomes and a responsible process.

## 4. Partner with an advisory firm that advises on all product solutions and advocates blended solutions

It is not common practice at present for advisory firms to advise on all product solutions. For example, fixed term annuities account for only 5 per cent of advised retirement business, yet this product provides a combination of certainty and flexibility and can be used to mitigate sequence risk. Advisers are also reluctant to advise a blended solution, choosing instead to recommend the binary decision of annuity or drawdown. However when a customer is moving from a secure DB environment to a potentially more risky DC environment a blend of solutions, which may include capital guarantees or income guarantees, can play an essential role in mitigating risk.

## 5. Choose a partner that members recognize and trust, with the financial strength to stand by their advice recommendations

DB transfers by their very nature are complex. Selecting an experienced advisory partner who is recognized and trusted by your employees and is financially strong should anything go wrong is a sensible step.

## 6. Ensure fair value

It's essential that a transfer value provides fair value for the scheme member to ensure, where the circumstances are right for the individual to transfer, a good outcome is delivered. The consequence of this is that it will deliver benefit for the scheme sponsor by reducing scheme liabilities. If the transfer values do not represent fair value, then for most members the advice will be to remain in the scheme. This therefore benefits no-one except perhaps the advice partner.

We believe that by following these simple steps it is possible to create a responsible and fair process that handles the inevitable requests for DB transfers in a robust way that ensures good customer outcomes and a win-win solution for all.

---

As the Head of Distribution, Steve Lewis is a member of the LV= Retirement Solutions leadership team that has transformed the business over the last five years from being a niche annuity provider to a mainstream retirement business. The delivery of new propositions to market has been a key focus of his work, particularly through the transformation of the market resulting from the introduction of pension freedoms. LV= has been at the forefront of technology developments, providing client education and adviser support tools, and now launching groundbreaking on-line education and advice tools. Steve is a retirement specialist with considerable industry experience, working closely with advisers and providers in the market. To find out more about LV= Corporate Solutions and how they can help you, call the LV= Corporate Solutions team on 08000 850 260, email Corporate.Solutions@lv.com or visit LV.com/corporatesolutions

# Insured solutions

## 4.4

*Guy Freeman at Rothesay Life discuss the potential for transferring a series of complex risks through a bulk annuity.*

Defined benefit pension promises are increasingly a legacy issue for company directors and their shareholders. The aspiration for these companies is to wind up the pension trust and secure with an insurance company the pension promises made to any current and former employees who are members of the employer's scheme. This relieves the employer of the associated complex risks and burdens that come with running such an off-balance sheet entity and allows the directors to return their full focus to the business.

## What risks are shareholders running?

When the company made a pension promise to an employee, it entered into a long-term commitment that carries a number of complex risks including:

- Longevity: What if members live longer than expected and more pension payments than expected are made?
- Marital status: Most schemes provide a pension benefit to a surviving spouse when a member dies. What if they have younger than expected spouses? What if more are married than was expected?
- Inflation: Benefit payment amounts typically increase annually according to emerging inflation
- Interest rates and investment risk: Companies are required to provide funding for their defined benefit schemes to meet the expected cost of the benefits over time

Managing this particular mixture of risks is not a core skillset for many company directors, and distracts from the day-to-day business of running the company. How can these risks be reduced or removed?

To secure the benefit promises made to members, the pension fund can purchase a bulk annuity contract from a UK regulated life insurance company. A bulk annuity contract will contain a list of individuals and their pension amounts. Each month, the insurer will pay out the requisite pension benefits for each of the members that are alive. The insurer therefore takes on all the risks listed above for the members covered by the contract.

## How do you buy a bulk annuity?

To buy a bulk annuity the pension fund would engage a specialist adviser to solicit quotations from the insurance market. At the moment there are around seven insurers who would be interested in quoting for a bulk annuity for a UK pension fund. The adviser helps the pension fund select the appropriate insurer for their particular needs, usually after a few rounds of bidding, and a contract between the pension fund trustees and the insurer is then signed. The required premium is paid to the insurer soon after, usually by transferring assets such as gilts but occasionally by a wire transfer of cash.

The process to go from initial approach to the insurance market to securing the contract typically takes around three months if the historical pension records have been well kept, the benefits payable to scheme members are well defined and the fund is clear on their aims for the transaction.

## Can't afford the full premium?

The majority of pension funds don't have enough assets to purchase a bulk annuity covering the full pension promises to all members, and would therefore need a contribution from the sponsoring employer to bridge the gap between scheme assets and the insurance premium. If the employer is not able or willing to pay this, the pension fund could buy a bulk annuity that covers only part of the pension promises, usually by only purchasing cover for a subset of the scheme's membership. Typically the pension fund might insure the members who are currently receiving a pension and exclude the younger members who have not yet reached retirement age. In this case the bulk annuity contract is called a 'buy-in' and the insurer makes payments to the pension fund trustees rather than directly to the insured members. It is effectively an investment of the pension fund, and removes the risks listed in the section above in respect of the members covered by the contract.

## Time to wind up

Where the employer can afford to insure the whole scheme, a bulk annuity is secured to cover all of the pension promises made to all scheme members, funded by the existing assets in the fund plus the final contribution from the employer.

The bulk annuity transfers to the insurer the responsibility to pay scheme members their pension promises, and the members of the pension fund receive insurance policies in their own name. The pension fund is then able to wind-up and close down. This process of purchasing a bulk annuity to cover all the scheme benefits and subsequently transferring the insurance to members' own names is called a pension 'buy-out'.

> **How big is the market?**
>
> Over the 5 years 2010 to 2014, the market for pension fund buying bulk annuities has totalled £35.8bn.
>
> Transactions larger than £100m premium accounted for 76% of the total market. Over the period, pension funds have transacted with 10 different insurers

## Certainty of economics for buy-outs

Given the typically large size of the final contribution into the pension fund to facilitate buy-out, the employer board will often have hands-on involvement in the process of completing the transaction. Usually the board will have approved a buy-out as long as the contribution required from the employer is within a pre-agreed budget. The process is typically one of trying to secure a buy-out using the fund's assets plus a fixed amount of additional funding from the company. In addition the board will typically want to know that this final payment really is final, and there will be no subsequent demands for further funding in future. This presents two issues:

1 The required contribution for the annuity tends to be a volatile number. The value of the scheme's assets and the insurer's premium don't tend to move in line with each other, resulting in a variable gap to be funded by the employer. An insurer might quote an affordable premium only to find that the shortfall has increased beyond the budget before all parties are ready to sign the contract.

2 To achieve a wind-up without further costs it is important to ensure that the insurance exactly matches the pension fund liabilities and that a sensible budget is held for all other potential costs of wind-up eg legal fees.

The good news is that insurance companies have developed solutions to resolve both of these issues and give companies the cost certainty they need to proceed to buy-out.

## Removing volatility between the premium and the scheme's asset value

It is possible for the insurer to define their premium in terms of a portfolio of gilts, meaning that the premium only moves over time in line with changes in the value of the gilt portfolio. This not only provides the scheme and the employer with complete transparency over movements in premium levels, it also means that if the scheme invests their assets in the same portfolio of gilts, the gap between the scheme assets and the premium becomes fixed, giving the employer certainty over their required level of contribution during the period between selecting an insurer and the actual policy inception date. The cost of the transaction can simply be met through the delivery of the gilt portfolio together with any coupons.

## Ensuring that the insurance exactly matches the liabilities

When a pension fund is fully bought-out, the requirement to provide pensions to all the scheme members is transferred in full to the insurer. It is therefore vital that each member's benefits are precise and well defined. Despite many funds spending time and effort cleansing their data over recent years, the task of ensuring that all eligible members are included in the data set with their correct benefits can be both time consuming and costly. These uncertainties in the benefits to be insured may not be resolved for several years after transacting the initial buy-in. This causes two problems; it delays the wind-up and eventual settlement of the scheme until all these issues are resolved, and means that the sponsor doesn't achieve certainty of the final cost for potentially several years.

To resolve these issues, pension funds and corporate sponsors have sought to secure 'all-risks' buyouts. Under this structure, the insurer takes on risks such as longevity and investment risks as for a regular buyout, but also takes on a number of additional risks. These include data errors, missing members, incorrect interpretation of the Trust Deed and Rules when administering member's benefits, future legislative changes and the risk that in future, equalization of GMP benefits must be undertaken using a different methodology to that adopted by the Trustees. Using this transaction approach, the company and trustees would only pay a single premium at the inception of the policy. An additional benefit of this methodology is a quick and full settlement of liabilities, as there is no additional management time and effort required between buy-in and wind-up, and the pension scheme is removed from the corporate pension accounting balance sheet at a much earlier stage.

Guy Freeman is Co-Head of Business Development at Rothesay Life, one of the leading providers of regulated insurance solutions in the UK market for pensions de-risking, making payments of around £700m a year from over £19 billion of insurance contracts. In 2015, Rothesay Life received over £2.5 billion of bulk annuity premiums from pension funds to date (2014: £1.7bn). This strong growth has been achieved through the steady accumulation of pension scheme clients and significant strategic acquisitions.

Existing Rothesay Life clients include the pension schemes and members associated with such names as RSA, British Airways, Lehman Brothers, Rank, Uniq, General Motors, the MNOPF (Merchant Navy Officers Pension Fund), InterContinental Hotels, Philips, GKN and the Civil Aviation Authority.

Telephone: +44 (0)20 7770 5300 E-mail: Guy.Freeman@Rothesaylife.com
www.rothesaylife.com

# PART FIVE
# Scheme design

# PART FIVE
## scheme design

# How to integrate everyone into a coherent scheme

## 5.1

*Auto-enrolment represents a big moment of change for pensions. Is it just another layer of administration? Or could you streamline all the benefits you offer, asks Carole Nicholls at Nicholls Stevens.*

The arrival of auto-enrolment means that all employers must review current and future pension provision for their employees. In my experience of working with SMEs over the last 25 years I have observed that most businesses have developed pension provision for their employees on an ad hoc basis. Many employers originally offered defined benefit schemes. Over the last 10 years most of these schemes have been closed either to new members or to future accrual. The defined benefit schemes have been replaced by defined contribution schemes either trust-based or group personal pensions.

What I see on a day to day basis when working with smaller companies is that many employers operate two or three schemes, a trust-based scheme now usually defined contribution and a Group Personal Pension or Stakeholder arrangement for newer entrants. Entry to some of these schemes may be restricted by age or employment status.

In some organizations, the Directors may have their own self-invested personal pension and frequently I see instances where employers have been willing to contribute to individual employee's personal pensions resulting in a plethora of administration. in one company I was recently advising there were 45 payments every month to different insurance companies.

Now, through the introduction of auto-enrolment, the Government are forcing employers to consider the pension provision for eligible jobholders. It would be so easy just to add yet another scheme to the existing plethora of schemes, or to add all eligible jobholders to a basic auto-enrolment scheme, such as NEST. However, we at Nicholls Stevens are pointing out to our clients that this is a unique moment to review the provision of pension benefits within their organization and to see if there is not a cheaper more streamlined solution for the future.

We propose a four-stage process: preparation, analysis, review and action.

# Stage 1: Preparation

Before seeking advice you need to become familiar with your own circumstances and review the following:

## *Understanding your own situation*

### 1   When will auto-enrolment happen for my company?

You need to be aware of the time scale for implementing the changes. If you do not already know your date for auto-enrolment this you can check by visiting the Pension Regulator's website: www.thepensionsregulator.gov.uk/employers/staging-date. Once you know this date you know the time scale for implementing any changes. You need to start work on this at least 12 months in advance of your staging date.

### 2   How many of my employees will be affected?

You need to know how many of your employees will fall into the category of eligible jobholders and must therefore be automatically enrolled into a qualifying scheme. The definition of an eligible jobholder is 'an employee aged between 22 and the state pension age, working in the UK and has qualifying earnings above £10,000 pa'. The eligibility criteria need to be assessed on every pay day and therefore there can be a sting in the tail because an employee earning less than £10,000 per annum may in fact be eligible to be auto-enrolled in a week or month when he or she receives a bonus or works a great deal of overtime.

### 3   What about the remainder of my employees?

The remainder of your employees will either be non-eligible jobholders, these employees are aged under age 21 or over state pension age, and/or they have lower earnings, within a band of £5,824–£10,000 per annum. These employees have a right to ask to opt into the scheme and if they do so, you will have to make contributions. Finally there is a group of entitled workers with earning less than £5,824 pa who can ask to join a scheme but for whom you are not responsible for paying a contribution.

## Understanding the cost of auto-enrolment

**1** Once you have worked out the number of employees who are likely to be included in auto-enrolment you can use the minimum employer contribution figures of 3 per cent of qualifying earnings to work out the approximate cost of future pension. In this rough calculation I would advise including the non-eligible jobholders so you know the maximum expenditure.

**2** In addition to this basic cost there will also be administration charges. Even if you are running existing schemes, in the future there will be more members of the schemes, so costs will undoubtedly rise. It is vital to consider how much extra you are prepared to pay for professional advice and administration because this decision will play a key role in your decision making for the method of future provision of benefits.

# Stage 2: Analysis

You now need to look at the current scheme or schemes you run. You do not need to have an in depth knowledge of pensions to undertake this review. You are looking at the schemes from your point of view and asking a number of questions which revolve around the cost of running the existing arrangements and whether they meet the needs of yourself and your employees.

## a) What type of scheme or schemes do we run?

If you still run a defined contribution scheme these are trust-based and bring with them a large amount of administration and compliance work. They are costly to run in time and money. If you open these schemes up to increased membership you will undoubtedly be increasing costs particularly if you are now included transient workers.

If you are already running a group stakeholder or personal pension arrangement this may be a more suitable vehicle to use to satisfy the auto-enrolment requirements for all or the majority of employees particularly as the flexibility of personal pensions means that the leaving service process is not an administratively expensive exercise. However, if you have run the scheme for some time, it may need updating. It may be possible to reduce the charges, increase the fund options and provide, you the employer with a more efficient internet-based payment system.

### (b) How many eligible jobholders belong to the current scheme or schemes?

Doing this calculation is a useful exercise because it helps you put a figure on future costs. If a large number of eligible jobholders are already members of your schemes then the increase in costs is unlikely to be great.

### (c) What are the costs of running the scheme?

If you run a trust-based scheme, ever increasing compliance requirements mean that you have to rely on expensive professional help. There are heavy administration costs when members leave service and retire. In comparison if you offer a Group Personal Pension, on leaving service the employee takes the plan and the employer has no further administration costs or liabilities.

### (d) Will your existing scheme qualify for auto-enrolment?

This will be a question to ask your advisers in Stage 3 but in most cases a scheme can qualify subject to a small rule amendments or alteration of, say the definition of pensionable salary.

### (e) Do you think the current scheme or schemes will fit the needs of the employees in the future?

You need to review the existing scheme under three headings: contributions, flexibility and investment.

#### Contributions

How much do you pay into the existing schemes, is it more than the minimum contribution for auto-enrolment? If it is then this should be retained as it will serve as a differentiator in future for recruitment purposes. Similarly if you currently offer a salary sacrifice facility or a lump sum death in service benefit all this will be appreciated by the employee of the future and needs to be retained.

#### Flexibility

The employee of the future is likely to move jobs and employment status and needs a flexible pension plan, which moves with them. An employee is therefore, likely to appreciate a personal pension rather than membership of an occupational scheme, unless it is a defined benefit scheme.

## Investment options

The amount of an employee's future pension is now almost totally dependent upon investment return, so investment choice is vital. Many schemes which I review offer a very restricted fund choice. Post auto-enrolment, within your scheme there will need to be a default fund for those who do not make an investment choice, but also a wide range of risk rated funds for those who are making a personal selection.

## (f) Do you think that you can cope with the future administration of the scheme?

Going forward the administration of the scheme to comply with auto-enrolment is as much about good pay roll software as pension administration. If you offer the existing scheme to an increased membership these administration costs are likely to rise.

# Stage 3: Review or initiation

When you enter this stage you will have done your preparation work on your existing schemes, you will know; the numbers of employees involved, the costs and whether you think your schemes will be fit for purpose in the future.

If you are currently paying into individual employees personal pensions, I would recommend you cease doing this and introduce a group personal pension arrangement which can be treated as a qualifying scheme. If contributions are going into a SIPP arrangement for Directors it may be appropriate to retain this and for them to opt out of any auto enrolment scheme.

However, you may have no provision in which case you start with a clean sheet. You will need to decide whether you want to establish a 'qualifying scheme' which offers better benefits than the minimum Government requirement or rely on a scheme such as NEST.

## Getting advice

If you have an adviser for your existing scheme before automatically including all employees I suggest you take this opportunity to ask at least one alternative adviser to report on the scheme.

The pension scheme of the future will be a defined contribution scheme most probably a group personal pension. The administration and premium collection should be streamlined and the legislation less onerous but investment advice will be vital. A good employer will want to offer his employees access to independent financial advice.

Therefore, you may like to take advice from a firm which specializes in advising SME companies or one with experience of running group personal pension arrangements and ideally can give independent investment advice to members who may need this. Having this option will be particularly important with the advent of 'pension freedoms' which means that your employees will have a myriad of choices to make at retirement and will definitely need financial advice.

If you have no scheme you will need to ask a number of advisers to report on the options open to you and make sure that you not only investigate Insurance Company solutions but also schemes offered by organizations such as NEST, NOW and People's Pension.

## Stage 4: Taking action

### 1 Appoint or retain an adviser

You will need to agree fees and the services to be provided.

### 2 Modify the existing scheme to make it a qualifying arrangement

This process may require rule changes to a trust deed or changes to contracts of employment.

### 3 Introduce a new scheme

If you are going to close an existing scheme and introduce a new one, or if you have no scheme and you and are introducing a new one, time is of the essence. If you are using an insurance company scheme notice of at least 6 months will be essential and I advise one year. You may wish to bring forward your staging date so that you can get your scheme in force well before the rush of schemes auto enrolling in 2016–17. It is estimated that at least 610,000 employers will be seeking to implement schemes in this period.

You must leave time to consult with employees or unions, change contracts of employment and carry out presentations and surgeries.

## How to Integrate Everyone into a Coherent Scheme

**Preform Packaging Ltd**

### Introduction
35 employees

### Current Pension provision
In 2006 a Group Personal Pension scheme was introduced.
**Section A contribution:** employer 8% of P60 earnings, employee 5% of P60 earnings.
**Section B contribution:** employee 3% of P60 earnings, matched by the employer up to 5% of P60 earnings.
20 employees are in no scheme.

### Preparation for auto-enrolment
The employer staging date is July 2016.
The employer used our check list to understand his situation.
We carried out our review.
As the GPP was out of date we put the scheme out for tender.
The existing provider was able to offer more competitive terms on the understanding that we included all employees except the packers who would be auto-enrolled into NEST. The contribution level meant that the scheme was qualifying for auto-enrolment purposes.

### Action
The employer will introduc the improved GPP scheme. Presentations and surgeries will take place to encourage new membership.
Premium collection is internet-based and the insurance company has offered an internet-based tool to help the employer remain compliant for auto-enrolment.

### 4 Check all software

You need to make sure that all premium collection systems are in place and have been tested before auto-enrolment commences for you.

# The outcome of using the auto-enrolment check list

We have recently been through the review checklist with one of our clients and here are the results:

Carole Nicholls is the Managing Director of Nicholls Stevens (Financial Services) Limited. The fee-based firm was established in 1986 and specializes in retirement advice to SMEs and individuals. The administration team of 14 is situated in Bristol but there is also a small office in London and Nicholls Stevens administer schemes across the UK. Nicholls Stevens is a boutique rather than a supermarket and so clients can expect a bespoke service at a reasonable price.

Carole is a Fellow of the Personal Finance Society and a Fellow of the Chartered Insurance Institute. She is committed to improving standards within the industry and served as national president of the Personal Finance Society in 2007 she also frequently speaks at conferences and has written numerous articles and books on pensions matters including The Pensions Jigsaw.

Further details: www.nichollstevens.com

# Pensions for top performers

5.2

*As an up-and-coming enterprise, how do you start to think about creating a pensions strategy to keep your team together, asks Ronald Olufunwa at Westminster Wealth.*

You have spent a decade of your life working for other people. You have demonstrated the ability to bring businesses to profit, and in some cases significantly so. You took a couple of ambitious members from your team and decided to set up a business, NewCo for yourself. Four years on, NewCo has carved out a niche for itself in the market, and have the real prospect of becoming a major player. Pensions were not your main consideration when you started up your new business, it was all about breaking even, broadening and deepening the client base and building the business income streams.

After a first nervous year, you had three years of solid growth, the numbers of employees within Newco have quadrupled as a result. The prospect of further expansion moves your thoughts to your organizational structure, and consolidating growth. Uppermost in your mind are the key staff in NewCo. They have made a difference to its operational capability or profitability. You are anxious to keep hold of them; you know one or two have been approached by a more established company across the way, with the promise of more money, a contributory pension, healthcare and an easier life. How do you compete?

This chapter is devoted to looking after the pension affairs of those who contribute most and matter most to the success of your business.

At the heart of your business will be your key employees. It makes sense that at the core of your exit strategy/retirement plans should be retirement planning for these people. The challenges in retaining staff are the same whether you run a family business, a business designed for sale or flotation, or a lifestyle business.

These broadly speaking are:

1 Suitability
2 Equitability

3 Differentiation
4 Affordability
5 Return on investment
6 DIY vs Advice

## Suitability

Before setting up a pension scheme for your business, you need to weigh up the different options available to you. You may already have an existing pension scheme, some of your staff may already have personal pensions. The scheme you choose to implement for key staff will also need to meet the minimum requirements of auto-enrolment.

By February 2018, all employers have to automatically enrol all of their 'jobholders' in a workplace pension scheme or in the National Employment Savings Trust (NEST) – a national defined contribution pension scheme. Job holders are defined as employees, temporary workers, directors employed under a service contract and agency workers who are considered to be employed by whoever is responsible for paying them.

## Equitability

Employees' sense of fair play in pay and benefits is a major factor in their sense of motivation and wellbeing at work. The 2012 Scottish Widows Pension Index [1] (which measures the current adequacy of provision by those who could and should be preparing financially for their retirement) typifies adequate savers as married and in the latter part of their career in stable employment with large organizations.

Your typical 'key employee' is at the opposite end of the spectrum, being single or cohabiting, some with dependent children. They are in the midst of their career, working for smaller growing companies, and their earnings are relatively high. Unfortunately they are making little effort to save, and their expectations of retirement income and age may well be unrealistic.

NewCo Employees may not have a clear understanding of their relative importance if there is not a recognizable organizational pay structure and benefits. The typical result being all NewCo employees may feel that they are key to NewCo's success. Negotiating any ill feeling generated by a difference in pay and pension funding for key individuals compared to the rest of your workforce may prove challenging.

## Differentiation

How will you differentiate the provision for your key staff from other employees? How will this differentiation tie in with your statutory obligations around auto-enrolment for all staff and the abolition of a default retirement age?

Will the scheme provide the flexibility and differentiation of benefits your key staff members are likely to require? It's unlikely their retirement needs or attitudes to pension saving obligation will be the same.

An analysis of your employees on your payroll by age and occupation and location can give a fair indication as to their likely investment behaviour, which in turn can help you determine the likely investment complexity of the pension scheme.

Research by DCsions, a consumer insight specialist, highlights 10 intuitive segments of consumer's investment behaviour.

*Future Thinkers*
*Carpe Diems*
*Safe & Savvy*
*Grafters*
*Strategic Players*
*Health Hoarders*
*Navigators*
*Jugglers*
*Canny Movers*
*Untapped Potential*

The proactivity of each consumer type differs around financial planning and investment risk. The priorities vary from short-term (Carpe Diems) who as the name suggests are younger and don't view retirement savings as their main priority; to long-term (Future Thinkers) who want to make the best of their future pension contributions. Consequently a one-size-fits-all approach may not work.

Contrary to what you may think lower pension charges do not necessarily mean less flexibility. Stakeholder schemes are flexible from a contribution perspective though they have limited investment options.

If the majority of the workforce feel they do not have a great understanding of investments then there is little gain in paying higher management charges for a large investment universe. A stakeholder style pension with good default funds may suit a workforce with limited interest or knowledge in money matters. Even if key employees' investment knowledge is limited, an increased employer contribution into a stakeholder scheme (relative to other staff) can increase their sense of worth to the company, and your ability to retain them.

The important thing is to ensure an initial contribution entry point based on employee affordability (eg 1 per cent of gross monthly salary) for all staff members and a scheme and investment fund that suits the majority of your staff based on the age, occupation and likely understanding of financial matters. In such situations employee engagement will be low to start with. Clear communications to staff about the potential retirement outcomes of the Pension scheme will help them engage and match the scheme to their personal expectations for retirement.

Key staff may have an expectation of more sophisticated pension planning than a stakeholder scheme. For those employees a Group Self-Invested Personal Pension (GSIPP) or a Small Self-Administered Scheme (SSAS) can be an effective vehicle to deliver superior benefits to a chosen set of key employees who make your business more competitive.

Key employees will normally have proven themselves in a previous employment and have existing pensions. You will be more likely to be able to deliver healthy transfer terms for their existing pensions, and allow them to bring and any exotic investments they may hold them under one umbrella. Such schemes are generally suited to higher earners who have demonstrated the following investment behaviour as illustrated by the DCisions consumer segmentation model elements:

1. Future Thinkers – Interested in hearing how they can make the most of their contribution they proactively invest in more exotic investments
2. Strategic Players – Aware of the benefit of having a certain amount of risk in their pension portfolio, they see the big picture and make well informed decisions
3. Healthy Hoarders –likely have a pension with a former employer providing opportunity to consolidate multiple accounts and retirement solutions
4. Canny Hoarders- respond to information that helps them increase the return on their investments

They may be professionals such as architects, technical people with a specialized skill set, directors with operational, financial or sales prowess; or business owners.

## Affordability

According to the Office of National Statistics, workplace pensions had fallen to a new low by 2015. Just one in three (32 per cent of private sector workers) were saving into occupational schemes. Only a quarter of employers (26 per cent) reported to the Association of Consulting Actuaries that they were budgeting for the costs of auto enrolment. Can you as an Employer justify a greater outlay on a few key staff given that Auto enrolment is around the corner? What is the most cost effective method of doing this? It's important to quantify the costs and ways of reducing them:

1. The Government has attempted to quantify the cost of the administrative burden on employers in year one:

   250+ employees: £5 to £20 per employee in large firms

   50–249 employees: £15 to £30 per employee in medium firms

   5–49 employees: £25 to £50 per employee in small firms

   1–4 employees: £70 to £130 per employee in micro firms

2. Employers will need to check that they are satisfying the requirements in respect of minimum contribution levels for their employees. Employers with using personal pension style arrangements can self-certify that their scheme meets the minimum qualifying criteria provided the contributions are in accordance with one of the following tiers:

   **Tier 1:** A total minimum contribution of at least 9 per cent of pensionable pay (at least 4 per cent of which must be the employer's contribution). In this case contributions are only paid in respect of earnings in a defined band (currently £5,564 to £42,475).

   **Tier 2:** A total minimum contribution of at least 8 per cent of pensionable pay (at least 3 per cent of which must be the employer's contribution), provided that pensionable pay constitutes at least 85 per cent of earnings (the ratio of pensionable pay to earnings can be calculated as an average at scheme level

   **Tier 3:** A total minimum contribution of at least 7 per cent of all earnings (at least 3 per cent of which must be the employer's contribution).

   So by calculating the average earnings per employee you can verify the likely cost per of auto enrolment per employee, and chose the earnings definition that best ultimately suits your company's cash flow and pay structure.

3. Salary exchange is one of the most often overlooked mechanisms for enhancing pension contributions for staff, saving employee and employer national insurance, and meeting minimum auto enrolment levels for employers. It's an arrangement where your employees agree to give up some salary or bonus. The amount given up is used by you to provide a non-cash benefit to the employee.

As the employee is being paid less gross salary, you make an employer National Insurance Contribution (Er NIC) saving (of 13.8 per cent ) and the employee pays less tax and NICs. You can choose whether you share this saving with the employee, doing so for key staff will enhance their contributions to pension.

A SMART pension scheme is one that directs a proportion of Er NIC savings and all employees NIC and tax savings to pension significantly enhancing the employees' retirement fund

Once your employees engage with this mechanism and understand the benefits of salary exchange, you have the option of bringing other benefits on stream at reduced cost for the employee and yourself such as:

- child care vouchers
- bikes to work
- mobile phones
- buying annual leave

All of which will aid retention of existing staff and prove attractive to new staff

## Employee communications

A focus on costs can sometimes obscure the very real obligation of the employer's duty to ensure that all employees are given the right information and advice. Recent surveys show that employer tend to communicate about pension schemes only when employees join or when rules impact staff.

Focusing on key staff may prove challenging, as unfortunately the administrative burden that comes with auto-enrolment is the responsibility of employers.

1. You will need to ensure you have communicated with all staff about auto-enrolment and explained that they have the right to opt out if they wish. Employers must also report to the Pensions Regulator to confirm that they have complied with their auto-enrolment obligations.
2. You should bear in mind there are penalties for encouraging jobholders and newly recruited staff to opt out of auto-enrolment.
3. You will need to put in place administrative processes to identify auto-enrolment triggers for existing employees and new joiners eg
   - when jobholders turn 22
   - when they reach the minimum level of earnings
   - optional three-month waiting period to join
   - option to opt out after one month with a refund of contribution
   - option to re-enrol having one year of opting out
   - automatic re-enrolment after three years for non member

# Return on investment (ROI)

Pensions are designed to create a savings pot at retirement. Not only is it essential therefore that employees reviewing their pension fund performance on a regular basis, but that you as an employer regularly review their default investment options to ensure they are matching the performance expectations of your employees

The fact that auto-enrolment is a statutory obligation doesn't mean that you shouldn't have a return on your investment as an employer. Your corporate strategy around pension benefits may be simply to ensure staff place value on employer sponsored pensions; increasing workplace motivation, retention of key staff; increased productivity, or attracting quality staff in a competitive business environment

Gradually phasing in an increase in employer contributions into pensions and bringing other NIC reducing benefits on stream in a measured and well communicated way, your employees will have a picture of an employer committed to valuing its employees and rewarding them with benefits designed to save them money or enhance their wellbeing.

How will you measure the return on your investment in their pensions?

Return on investment can be measured in several ways:

- Via engagement with the Pension Scheme – evaluating participation levels and contributions over and above any employer matched amount
- Survey, cheap and effective surveys can be conducted that will give you an insight into the perceived value of the pension scheme and motives behind staff participation or non usage of pension scheme (using websites like www.surveymonkey.co.uk)
- Salary exchange benefits lend themselves readily to a 'pounds saved' comparison against the value if they had bought the benefits themselves
- Is the choice of Pension Provider perceived as enhancing or detracting from your Pension offering
- Do their online systems reduce the administrative burden of auto enrolment; or enhance your ability to measure KPIs? Some pension providers include HR software that measures some of these KPI as part of their pension package
- By recording key performance indicators (KPI), such as staff turnover, sickness absence, and productivity; comparisons can be made between before and after implementation of pension benefits,

## DIY vs advice

### DIY

If you are contemplating sourcing a pension scheme for your key staff, considering factors such as affordability and return on investment will help you deliver good outcomes for your corporate objectives and considering factors like suitability, differentiation, equitability and employee communications will help you deliver good outcome for your employees savings.

A summary of issues you may wish to discuss directly with pension providers and their appointed representatives is:

- The level of funding you are prepared to give as an employer
- How will you consult with employees regarding which scheme you intend to offer?
- Will the scheme match the growth of your company? If not can you easily change to a different provider? Or will the pension scheme be future proof?
- Are there any investments you would like to invest via pension in the future as a company eg commercial property (or areas you'd like to avoid)?
- The costs, charges and penalties involved in the scheme – are they competitive?
- Do you want the pensions to be easily portable?
- What will the charges be for those who leave your organization?
- Will your pension scheme be auto-enrolment ready scheme will comply with future legislative changes eg auto-enrolment, and abolition of the default retirement age?

Opting to do it yourself may be cheaper in the shorter term but it is not for everyone. The Pensions Regulator produces helpful guides for businesses around auto enrolment.

### The need for advice

A professional independent adviser will help you create and develop a comprehensive list of requirements. They will help you negotiate pension legislation such as auto-enrolment, and the abolition of a default retirement age. It's important that your selection process is robust and documented. This will aid further down the line if employees question your choice of scheme and benefit levels, or the retirement outcomes of the scheme. It will also be of great help to any key employee wishes to understand your companies corporate needs and objectives.

# The benefits of using a corporate financial adviser are:

## Technical expertise

- They will be able to create a bespoke solution for your company
- They will be able to give you industry /sector specific information
- They will be able to tell you what is competitive offering in your market sector

## Cost

- The Retail distribution review has made it easier for Employers to see what you being charged for by way of advice
- The administrative cost of auto enrolment can reduced
- Best positioned to help you maximise savings through salary exchange

## Implementation

- They can research the whole of market
- They can implement schemes quickly and cost effectively
- They will document accountabilities for all aspects of running the scheme

## Communications

- A corporate financial adviser can help you tie our corporate objectives to your pension funding
- Well positioned to conduct appropriate surveys of employee needs, and perceived value of benefits
- They can assist with complex corporate financial planning eg debt raising and exit strategies. or facilitate commercial premises via pensions
- Provide advice to key staff, eg facilitate in specie contributions into pensions or enhanced pension contributions
- Provide independent financial advice to all staff – Corporate advisers will typically be part of a team who have other advisers who can perform basic holistic planning, and it may be useful to include holistic financial advice to employees as a condition of scheme implementation. Employees would appreciate access to professional advice from an independent financial adviser irrespective of whether it is basic financial housekeeping, retirement planning advice or mortgage advice. Employees are very much occupied by the present financial challenges like raising their next mortgage rather than future ones like retirement planning,

## Scheme Design

A well-structured pension scheme can provide a strategic bridge between your corporate objectives, the needs and ambitions of your key staff and the wellbeing and motivation of all your employees.

> Ronald Olufunwa is a Corporate IFA who specializes in creating and delivering sophisticated corporate financial planning to entrepreneurs and their businesses. His expertise allows him to deliver creative solutions to the manufacturing, medical, retail, technological and charitable sectors. Clients value his holistic focus on their businesses and commitment to long term strategies that add value.
>
> His professional advice is provided not only to Westminster Wealth clients but also to those of external professionals such as solicitors, tax technicians and accountants.
>
> Ronald has made appearances on TV and radio including The Money Programme and Radio Sussex. He is married with two young children and lives in Brighton. Ronald's passions include poetry, oriental literature, modern art, supporting Liverpool Football Club and languages – he is slowly learning German. Ronald is also a Director and Trustee of Brighton & Hove Community & Volunteer Forum, a Governor and Treasurer of a London school, and a Grants UK Storytelling Finalist.

# How to set up an international scheme

5.3

*Carl Hansen at BWCI reviews where and how international plans are now being run*

In practice, most international pension plans are established in one of the world's international finance centres in order to provide greater flexibility. US multinationals have historically favoured Bermuda or the Cayman Islands. For UK multinationals, the obvious choices are Guernsey, Jersey, or the Isle of Man.

The ideal location for an international pension plan is a reputable international finance centre with political and economic stability. Investment income and benefit payments should be exempt from local taxation. Enabling legislation should allow for design flexibility, especially on benefit levels and forms of payment. Efficient plan establishment is aided by helpful regulatory authorities and an appropriate (but not excessive) level of regulation.

UK multinationals can set up plans for international staff under the provisions of Section 615(6) of the UK Income and Corporation Taxes Act 1988. This has the advantage that the pension plan could be controlled and managed in the UK alongside the domestic UK pension plan.

## Development over the years

Historically, many international pension plans were set up on a defined benefits basis, to mirror the provisions of the multinational's home pension plan with minor adjustments to reflect the overseas service. As a variation, a 'base country' approach has sometimes been adopted, whereby a base country is determined for each of the international staff with benefits provided on the same basis as local staff working in that base country, regardless of where the international staff are posted. However, defined benefit structures can be inflexible and complex to administer.

In common with worldwide trends, most new international pension plans are set up on a defined contribution basis. A flexible defined contribution or hybrid international pension plan can supplement or replace an existing defined benefit plan on a more cost effective basis.

Another trend is to establish international pension plans on a 'master trust' approach, so that a number of different plans can be provided within a single trust. This can prove more cost effective than setting up separate trusts. It can also provide a central investment vehicle for local pension plans operated by subsidiaries within the group that do not have suitable local vehicles.

## Funding

Funding rules for international pension plans generally allow flexibility. Tax issues in some countries, most notably the US, can cause difficulty for plan design and administration. US tax rules typically defer taxation on assets saved for retirement in one of only a few US tax qualified arrangements. Also, US taxpayers are taxed on worldwide income regardless of where they live. As a result, contributions to an international pension plan (both employer and employee) on behalf of a US taxpayer member are generally taxable income when they are made.

Some employers have taken the position of excluding US taxpayers from international pension plans in order to avoid adverse tax consequences. Some service providers will also exclude US taxpayers to avoid administrative difficulties and reporting requirements under the Foreign Account Tax Compliance Act (FATCA). Other employers have decided to not fund international pension plans that include any US taxpayers.

While an unfunded approach may have tax benefits for a limited number of members, it leaves all members in the plan with no security in the event of employer insolvency. Also, a lack of plan assets will probably deter some service providers with asset-based fees or less transparent charging structures.

An alternative to an unfunded approach is to fund for all members except US taxpayers and any other members with adverse tax issues. Administration systems should now be sufficiently sophisticated to handle separate classes of members.

## Trusteeship and administration

Central to the establishment and operation of a successful international plan is the appointment of a suitable trustee and administrator. The trustee should be based in the chosen international finance centre, in order to demonstrate control and management there to avoid taxation or regulatory problems in the home territory. Several international finance centres specialize in the provision of trustee services. The better regulated international finance centres have not only introduced their own trust law but have also introduced legislation to regulate professional trustees. Some multinationals wish to retain more control by forming a separate trustee company in the international finance centre.

Investment management need not be carried out in the plan location. It is increasingly common for international pension plans to invest in the pooled funds of major financial institutions.

## Establishment and operation

An international pension plan is typically established by means of a trust deed and rules, structured to comply with local laws in the chosen jurisdiction. The documentation should be submitted for approval (or confirmation of exemption from local taxation, as applicable) to the tax office where the plan is being established and any other relevant regulatory body there.

Before proceeding, it is also advisable to investigate the taxation and regulatory position for the international pension plan in each of the locations where the intended members are based. Employer contributions to international pension plans are typically effectively tax deductible for the employer as an employment expense. However, some countries (for example the US as mentioned previously) will view employer contributions as taxable income to employees when made. Employee contributions to an international pension plan are not usually tax deductible, but it may be possible to make them tax effective depending on individual circumstances. If employer contributions would be taxable on the employee as a benefit in kind then it may be necessary for such tax to be recompensed by the employer.

The new generation of defined contribution international pension plans are very flexible to meet the needs of a variety of employer types and sizes. Employer contributions can be uniform or vary according to home country, host country, age, service, or a variety of other criteria. Members can choose from a wide range of investment funds in various currencies to fit their own circumstances. Most plans provide some sort of a lifestyle fund or strategy as a default option for those employees wanting less involvement in the selection of their investments.

Member communication is important to the success of any pension plan, and is particularly important for international pension plans, where the members are physically remote both from head office and from the trustees and administrators. Most plans now centralize communications via a dedicated plan website with secure access to benefit and membership information, possibly in more than one language. Websites for defined contribution plans typically handle investment changes and enable retirement modelling.

## Plans established under contract

Many international insurance companies and investment fund providers now also provide services to international pension plans. These companies will arrange a contract with the employer to provide services to the plan in exchange for holding and managing the plan's funds.

Contract-based arrangements are intended to be a cost-effective approach for an employer to set up and operate an international pension plan, especially for a small number of members. However, there may be some less transparent costs involved in the form of asset-based fees taken from the investment returns. In a defined contribution arrangement, this can mean significantly lower retirement balances for members over the course of their career.

Plans established under contracts are generally less flexible than those set up using a trust. The permitted plan provisions and investments tend to be limited to fit within the terms of the provider's standard contract with minimal individual tailoring allowed.

While a trust is a separate entity from the employer and any provider, a contract-based arrangement remains the property of the employer and the asset is the provider's policy. The plan members therefore have employment and retirement benefit provision risk concentrated in their employer, and there is also some risk of loss of capital on the insolvency of the provider.

## Summary

International pension plans are an increasingly important part of the armory of the human resources director in meeting the employment needs of a globally mobile workforce. They remain an elegant and tax efficient way to provide retirement benefits for employees who might otherwise have little or no formal pension provision due to their working location or their mobile lifestyle. The demand for international pension plans is expected to continue to increase, as companies increasingly find the need to conduct their businesses internationally.

> Carl Hansen is International Director at the BWCI Group in Guernsey in the Channel Islands. He qualified as a Fellow of the Society of Actuaries (US) in 1996 and earned a Diploma in International Employee Benefits in 2001. He specializes in international actuarial and other consultancy services to multinational employers. During his career, Carl has had in depth experience with retirement plans and other benefits issues in the US and many other jurisdictions around the world, including establishing and implementing international pension plans.k

# PART SIX
# Risk management

## *"Delivering value through good governance"*

**PTL is a specialist and award winning Independent Pensions Trustee company. Our team deliver expert pensions governance advice to businesses across the UK.**

We believe that as professional pension scheme governors we need to lead from the front. Our commitment is to remain at the centre of our industry and positioned to influence developments in the pensions market.

### We act for:

- Defined benefit schemes
- Defined contribution schemes
- Traditional trust based schemes
- Contract based schemes
- Group personal pension plans
- Open schemes
- Closed schemes
- Schemes in wind up and schemes in transition
- Charities
- We also act for non-pension entities

### Why chose PTL?

**People** - we aim to attract and retain the best.

**Experience** – we have extensive experience of acting as a professional trustee and governing pension schemes.

**Team** – we work as a team on all appointments, so clients get the benefit of our collective expertise.

**Diverse** – the team come from varied backgrounds within the industry, giving us a rare breadth and depth of knowledge and experience that our clients can benefit from

**Executive style** – most of our clients want more than an 'expert for hire'. They need us to help them to achieve their objectives. Our hands-on style facilitates this.

# Tel: 0118 957 0610
# info@ptluk.com

**For our full range of services visit**

# www.ptluk.com

PTL was founded in 1994 and has offices in London, Reading, Birmingham and Leeds. Over the years we have helped numerous charities to enhance governance, reduce risk and manage their pension schemes more efficiently.

# Risks for scheme sponsors

## 6.1

*Pensions can give employers a nasty bite. Richard Butcher at PTL considers what protection to take.*

Imagine you had a box of snakes: big, small, dull or colourful but all venomous. Sticking your hand into this box would be a very silly but also dangerous thing to do. That said, unless you feed them the snakes will get hungrier and more aggressive. Leaving them a couple of days like that would be even sillier and even more dangerous. It's a box of risk and the longer you ignore it the greater the risk gets.

Imagine a workplace pension scheme: big or small, mostly dull, maybe not venomous but no less a box of risks – process, investment and liability risks. Ignoring those risks would be a very silly and dangerous thing to do and the longer you ignore them the greater the risks become.

Many businesses sponsor pension schemes already but if yours doesn't it will do soon, thanks to the auto-enrolment regulations that require every employer from the largest to the smallest micro to automatically include their employees in a qualifying pension scheme by April 2017. Once you sponsor a pension scheme you have risks – maybe new risks – that need careful management. Ignore them at your peril.

Most UK employers offer Defined Contribution (DC) pension schemes although most employees in the UK continue to be in Defined Benefit (DB) pension schemes. The DB schemes tend, these days, to be confined to very large and older companies or statutory organizations like local authorities or those emanating from statutory schemes (many of the utilities for example). Very few employers are using DB schemes for auto enrolment. DB schemes have a risk profile all of their own and are, generally, regulated and managed to the hilt. For this reason, this article doesn't dwell on them. Instead it focusses on the less considered risks that come with the more widespread DC pension schemes.

All DC schemes work on the same principle. Money is paid in (usually from both employer and employee) in effect free of tax, is invested free of most taxes which results in a fund at retirement that can be used to provide retirement benefits. In the old days, before April 2015's Freedom and Choice changes, those benefits consisted mostly of an income. These days more or less anything goes.

The risks to your business stem from the type of scheme you use, its age and the charges applied and its efficiency. They also stem from how well informed your employees are and what they end up doing.

## The type of pension scheme you use

There are two types of DC pension scheme: contract and trust, although the first of these can be subdivided into single employer and multi-employer trusts. These should be considered separately.

### Contract-based:

Contract-based DC schemes are more commonly known as group personal pensions (or GPPs). In constitution they are a group of individual personal pension plans ie contracts between a provider and an individual member. The 'group' element has no legal meaning, it is merely a mechanism to achieve economy of scale.

### Single employer trust:

Trust-based pension schemes were common in the past (indeed before 1988 they were the only mechanism available for workplace pension schemes). They are a legal vehicle run by trustees appointed by the relevant employer. Employees become members on joining the scheme and have rights enforceable against the trustees.

### Multi-employer trust:

Multi-employer trusts are more commonly known as master trusts. They are also a legal vehicle run by trustees, but in this case the party creating the trust is a provider (perhaps an insurer, trade association, Union or anyone really). Employers participate in the trust. The aim, for master trusts, is that they achieve economies of scale that single employer trusts cannot.

## The risks inherent in each

All of these designs are at risk of being too old and or too expensive.
Over the years the cost of delivering a DC pension scheme has come down. This is due to improved and better use of technology. Tasks that 10 years ago took a clerk a week to complete can now be completed in nanoseconds by a computer. For this reason, if any scheme, whether contract or trust, is using infrastructure more than,

say, five years old or was priced more than five years ago it is likely to be too expensive. As the costs of DC schemes are invariably met by the member, this is not a good thing and exposes the employer directly (if a contract-based scheme) or indirectly (if a trust-based scheme) to the risk of employees litigating for neglect of duty of care.

This risk is mitigated, in part, in master trusts because, since April (a) a majority of their trustees must be independent of the sponsor and (b) the trustees have an explicit legal duty to consider whether the scheme offers good value. It is similarly mitigated in contract-based schemes because, again since April, they have had to have a governance function analogous to a trustee board assessing value for money. Finally, the risk is in part mitigated because no scheme used for auto-enrolment can cost more than 0.75 per cent (or a couple of similar charging models) a year. These mitigants, however, only reduce the employer's risk. They do not remove them entirely.

## Governance risk

In contract-based schemes high level governance is carried out by the provider. This aims to mitigate the risk of poor value for money, failing to deliver on mission and inappropriate default investment strategy. This, however, leaves the employer with the job of determining from time to time whether the provider is expensive, good for the job, or if they are delivering a package appropriate for their employees. Failure to have employer level governance of this nature exposes the employer to risk.

In trust-based schemes all of the functions of governance are carried out by the trustees, who, in turn, are indemnified by the employer (hence the risks sit indirectly with the employer). This risk can be mitigating by having effective trustees with relevant knowledge and experience.

In a master trust, the sponsor indemnifies the trustees and the trustees are required to be independent of the sponsor. As a consequence the only residual risk for the employer is that the master trust is a good one.

## Outcome risk

The proof of the pudding for any pension scheme has to be the benefits provided to the members when they need them.

While good governance and appropriate (perhaps low) charges provide the most efficient outcome for members they do not, in themselves, produce a good outcome. The main determinant of the outcome of a DC scheme is the volume of contributions paid in. Low contributions, no matter how efficiently looked after, will always produce low benefits.

The current generation of workers are the last that will see widespread DB pension schemes – a few will have had whole careers in a DB scheme, some will have some DB benefits, most will have wholly DC benefits. For the last two groups, this is the first generation that will retire with pensions significantly lower than those their parents enjoyed. This creates two risks for employers (a) that they (the employer) will not be able to manage their older workers out of the workforce as easily as in the past and (b) that employees, disappointed by the outcome of their pension, will litigate either because they weren't warned or aren't able to retire.

This risk can only be mitigated by a combination (in whatever weighting) of two things: higher contributions or effective engagement ie either make the contributions adequate or tell the member that they are inadequate.

## What should the responsible board do?

There are no easy answers to this question, in part because pension saving is very long term in nature and as a consequence the risks may not manifest themselves for years to come. There are, though, some rules of thumb.

Make sure the pension scheme you use for your employees is up to date. As a rule, if it's ever more than five years old, it is potentially out of date.

Make sure the pension provider is a good pension provider. Do some due diligence to ensure they are up to the job and sustainable.

Understand the governance structure: contract, trust or master trust, and make sure you do the bits of governance that fall to you.

Understand what benefits the contributions you pay will provide for your average employee. If they don't provide enough (a) pay more and or (b) make employees pay more and or (c) make sure they understand that they will have to fill the gap themselves if they are to have an adequate income in retirement. Don't forget that that aspiration, an adequate income in retirement, is good for you as well; it will allow you to manage people out of the workforce when it suits you as opposed to when it suits them.

If you run your own trust scheme, make sure the trustees are appropriately experienced, skilled and have sufficient time to do the job properly.

Pension risk is rarely fatal for a company but that's not to say that it can't do any damage. Pension schemes are a box of risks like many of the other things companies deal with. Those risks need careful management if they are not to bite.

> Richard Butcher is Managing Director of PTL, a firm that provides professional pension governance services to other companies. He is Chair of the PLSA's DC Council and sits on their board. He is also on the council of the PMI and a member of the DWP trustees panel and TPR's Dc practitioners panel.

# Systems and processes

6.2

*Employers are coming under increasing regulatory pressure to give a clear account of the risks in how they manage their pension schemes, says Bob Compton at Arc Benefits.*

With the passing of the Pensions Act 2008 all UK employers for the first time have by law a requirement to establish and facilitate workplace pension provision for its employees.

The effective date of this requirement depends on the size of your payroll at 1 April 2012, or if later when the new company was set up. The largest employers had to comply with effect from 1 October 2012, with employers of fewer than 30 people having what is known as a staging date between 1 January 2016 and 1 April 2017. Thus all employers with more than 30 employees will already have made decisions on its pension strategy, however a large number of smaller employers will be wondering what should be done.

There are a bewildering range of options and issues to consider, so much so that many employers will look for solutions that on the first sight may be simple and straight forward to implement, but could have long term ramifications for both the employee and employer. From the employer perspective non-compliance will lead to penalties imposed by the Pensions Regulator, that could range from a simple warning, fines ranging from £50 to £10,000 per day, warrants being issued (to search premises and take possession of content under S78 of Pensions Act 2004), to imprisonment of a director at the extreme.

With over 1.8m employers to regulate, the Pensions Regulator has outsourced the day-to-day management of auto-enrolment compliance to Capita (in the same way they run the London Congestion Charge).

So it is important to the company and individual Directors to take ownership of pensions strategy and risk.

The Pensions Regulator will require employers to provide information on their decision making process, where they believe the employer has been non-compliant with the regulations, so whether or not the employer or the Pensions Regulator is correct, having an audit trail of the employers decisions and process is important.

## Where to start

Older established organizations will already have a pensions history which may or may not be documented. With the changing of key executives over time and the move towards out sourcing specialist services, often the current management will have inherited positions without question. Smaller employers new to pension provision start with a clean sheet. However all employers should be clear where pension provision falls within their overall business and importance in delivering on objectives and profitability over the long term.

## Strategy

Whether you have existing pension schemes or are introducing a new scheme to comply with the auto-enrolment requirements, the employer should have a clear vision of what it needs to achieve from its pensions policy, and that vision should facilitate improving the efficiency and profitability of the business. Pensions are used as a recruitment and retention tool, but also now with the age discrimination regulations in place a well designed scheme can facilitate the natural retirement of employees whereas a poorly structured scheme may hinder retirement forcing the employer to instigate fit for the job assessments that could take many months and create bad feeling. Good strategy would be where the scheme design meets the employers and employees needs well. Bad strategy would be where the scheme that is implemented has the opposite effect. For example in a business that needs a regular supply of fresh thinking, it would be inappropriate to have a scheme that encouraged employees to hang on in work into their seventies!

## Key principles

Set out the key principles that the employer wishes to be guided by in delivering on its pension obligations. Principles could range from, complying with the minimum, right through to providing higher pensions than any other competitor regardless of cost? Same benefit package for all employees or tailored for role? Facilitate retirement by a target age, or retirement is of no concern as all employees will have left well before retirement is a consideration. Under employer control, or minimize employer involvement?

Clearly define policies, responsibilities, and structure. Where there is no existing pension provision, defining responsibilities and structure will be an iterative process as the pension scheme/s is/are developed and implemented. Different approaches, eg trust, master trust, contract, will shape the requirements on the employer for governance purposes.

In larger organizations more than one person will have responsibility for setting policy and implementation as legislation or the company evolves over time. Being clear on responsibilities within the organization, and how that inter relates with outsourced providers will reduce the opportunity for confusion, inaction, and increased costs. For smaller organizations often it will be the owner or managing director who will have sole responsibility, and the issue then is gaining knowledge and understanding to make informed choices. Most will look to an adviser for help.

> **Key points**
>
> For those starting the auto-enrolment process the Pensions Regulator website is a good place to start: www.thepensionsregulator.gov.uk. It provides clear guidance on the steps an employer should take but does not recommend what provider should be used.
>
> The Pensions Playpen website (www.pensionplaypen.com) is a very good source of information on options, and can provide basic advice for a fixed fee. Whist it will help employers through the auto-enrolment maze, it will not help with the ongoing responsibilities, the administration of which will depend on existing payroll capability, internal employer systems, and the interaction with the chosen pension provider.
>
> PLSA (the Pensions and Lifetime Savings Association, formerly NAPF) has a website area dedicated to providing unbiased information for employers of all sizes: www.plsa.co.uk.
>
> NEST (www.nestpensions.org.uk) is the government-sponsored work place pensions provider that by statute can be used by any employer wanting meet the auto-enrolment regulations. It was originally intended that NEST would be fully web-based, and would integrate with employer systems, but that has proved to be a step to far, so whilst NEST has web-based systems they do not systemize the employer's ongoing responsibilities.
>
> Other providers, insurance company contracts or schemes set up under master trusts such as The Peoples Pension and Now are also good sources of information, and they too have systems in place for managing member contributions, and complying with the startup regulations, but fall short of relieving the need for the employer to keep documenting processes and recording on going key decisions regarding their employees pension choices and options, communications, and re-enrolment of opt outs every three years.

## Other developments

Pension Freedoms were introduced by the Finance Act 2014 from April 2015. This introduces major changes to the way workplace pensions may operate and enables employees to have choice in the delivery of defined Contribution pension benefits at the point of 'drawing/crystallization/retirement'.

Most of the press activity following the change of policy has concentrated on the Employees new options and their ability now to make the 'wrong' decision on drawing down their pension. All Employers will need to develop their policy on whether to facilitate the drawdown options under their existing schemes, or to ignore the new freedoms.

For employers with legacy defined benefit pension schemes there is the possibility that a suitably developed offer for drawdown flexibility could help curtail widening scheme deficits. All decisions taken by the employer, and all communications will need to be recorded.

## The rise of centralized services

### Master trusts

In the UK, NEST was created by act of parliament to be a centralized pension provider for those Employers that were deemed too small for the Insurance and pensions industry to provide for.

Since the passing of the Pensions Act 2008 there has been a steady and increasing number of providers entering the Defined Contribution Master Trust market with well over 50 providers. A number will be invaluable institutions becoming household names in the coming years, but many have been created as a 'sticky' client retention mechanism and many will fall by the wayside. Getting truly independent advice on these will be difficult where the employers adviser runs its own master trust.

No one has yet witnessed the failure of a master trust, but the Regulator is starting to consider the implications of such scenarios, and believes in the longer term there will be consolidation of the better and more efficient.

The Government has introduced the concept of Independent governance committees. These are put in place by the operators of the master trust from 2015 and it is too early to establish how effective they will prove to be in delivering ongoing value and holding the operators to account.

Master trusts are increasingly attractive to employers as a way to reduce trustee and executive time spent on governance. However employers entering into master trust agreements give away controls that are often taken for granted under the current trust system. For example, the employer influence on communication with employees, input on investment options, giving the company a sense of 'our' scheme giving employees confidence they are working for a caring employer, may be more difficult to achieve.

Documenting any decision to go down the master trust route will be important including logging the information gleaned on costs, operating fees, and exit charges in arriving at a decision to appoint a master trust. Then how will the company oversee or not as the case may be whether or not the master trust delivers value to its employees in the coming years, and what influence will the company have with the trustees should things be not working out as well as anticipated/promised. And what would happen if the company chooses at a future date to change away from the master trust?

## *Fiduciary management*

In order to achieve reduced volatility of asset value to liabilities for defined benefit schemes more and more complex investment solutions have been developed. These have required more employer management time managing the complex investment strategies. As a result implemented fiduciary management services have been developed to enable the chosen consultant to manage these strategies without reference to the trustees or employer. As with master trusts many consultants now offer these services, calling into question their independence when advising the Trustees and Employer on these topics.

The service adds a layer of fees, but in return removes a layer of work, however control is removed. ie the trustees will have subcontracted active investment decisions to the outside organization, with or without the employers implicit agreement, and the manager could carry out investment practices that may not be in the employers interests. Employers need to ensure they retain a grip on costs, and have suitable independent appointment and monitoring processes in place and as with master trusts, that the exit route, should it be needed, is well documented including the terms for the transfer of assets.

These aspects will be more likely managed effectively if the employer has in place clear policies on its ultimate objectives in delivering work place pensions to its employees.

# Key systems and processes in managing and administering pensions

The Regulator's guidance on pension scheme governance both for defined benefit and defined contributions continues to evolve. The Pensions Act 2004 Section 249b makes it a legal requirement that appropriate internal controls are established. Trustees are expected to follow the guidance, but it is also the employer's responsibility where they have trustees or use a contract provider to ensure that they are satisfied these meet the appropriate test, and that they work with the Employers systems and processes.

As 'appropriate' is not defined, it really is only when something goes wrong that the Pensions Regulator will investigate. By then it will be too late to put in place controls. The employer should satisfy itself that it has systems and processes that will stand the test of outside examination.

Developing suitable systems for control purposes is fast becoming a key priority. Without suitable systems in place it will become increasingly difficult for employers to defend themselves against legal or regulatory action.

For example a large international firm with a US defined contribution plan, has been fighting a class action lawsuit against the company and the plan's record keepers (a well known fund manager) since 2006 for failing to control costs for the schemes participants, in a breach of fiduciary duty. The plan manager was chosen by the plan trustees, and despite the trustees perceived failure to exercise cost controls over the plan manager, it is the sponsoring employer that is embroiled in the action. The action has run on for nearly 10 years involving senior management in time and expense and if the case is lost will cost many millions in damages. New regulation applying from 1 October 2015 in the UK will make it easier for US style class actions to be brought in the UK.

In the UK legislation is now in place putting caps on fees levied by fund managers for Scheme default funds, fuelling the demand for transparency. Employers that put in place pension schemes or contracts that appear to be (with the benefit of hindsight) poor value will be exposed to potential litigation from disgruntled former employees. Decision making processes and the due diligence applied will be examined carefully in such circumstances. Having systems in place to record and retrieve is therefore essential.

Here is a starting list of headings to consider:

*Strategy*
*Policies*
*Processes*
*Practice*
*Actions*
*Reporting*
*Decisions*
*Monitoring*
*Review*
*Agents – Services, contractual agreements, and liability restrictions*

*Suppliers*
*Documentation*
*Training and development*
*Procedures for dispute resolution*
*Communications*
*Employee guidance/advice*
*Education*
*Compliance*
*Conflicts of interest*
*Risk management*

## Questions

**1** Are you clear from the company perspective who decides pensions policy?

**2** Question your existing pension policy, does it support the company operation?

**3** Are your executives or team clear on their responsibilities?

**4** Do you have out sourced services that meet your objectives and deliver value?

**5** 5Do you have an ongoing reporting mechanism that feeds back to 1?

Answers to these questions should be reported on an ongoing basis.

In summary, risk management and proper governance is at the heart of good management, and well thought out systems with effective and efficient monitoring will contain your costs and deliver valued benefits for your organization.

Bob Compton, is co-owner of ARC Benefits Limited, a Pensions Management and Governance specialist. Bob is a fellow of both the Pensions Management Institute, and Chartered Insurance Institute, with over 40 years consulting experience in the Pensions Industry. He is also co-author of 108½ Tips to Tame Your 'Pensions Beastie' a book on practical pensions management, and has acted as Pensions Policy Advisor to the British Chambers of Commerce.

# Employee risks

## 6.3

*In gaining more freedoms, employees will rely on more guidance in managing the risks for which they are now responsible, says Steve Lewis at LV= Corporate Solutions.*

The pension freedoms offer members much broader choice, flexibility and control over their retirement plans. However, this greater choice also brings increased responsibility and greater risk of making inappropriate decisions and makes it even more important that members seek guidance and advice to understand the risks involved and the potential options to mitigate them in retirement.

LV= offer financial advisers a retirement risk tool to help them identify and explain the risks. 'Hopscotch' explores the five main risk areas that members experience in retirement and also contains a questionnaire to assist advisers to assess attitudes to the retirement risks.

| Risk | Description | Potential mitigation actions |
|---|---|---|
| **Longevity risk** | The risk that a member lives a long time after retiring, exhausts their funds and is forced to rely on the state pension and other assets. Although it is an uncomfortable subject it is essential that members complete a health questionnaire and understand how long they may live. Research by the Institute of Fiscal Studies (IFS) showed that 59 per cent of over-55s had never thought about how long they will live in retirement. It is very common for members to assess their own longevity by considering when their parents died. The reality is that for the majority of members they will live longer lives than their parents. | Pension freedoms were available before the budget but only for a limited number of wealthy individuals who had at least £20,000 a year of guaranteed income. This was the minimum income requirement. The definition of income was restricted to state pension, defined benefits and lifetime annuity. To mitigate the risk of outliving their income, members should seek advice from a firm that has a fundamental advice principle of aiming to secure essential income requirements to pay the bills. The income could be from state pension, a partial DB benefit, a lifetime annuity or a fixed-term annuity. |

| Risk | Description | Potential mitigation actions |
|---|---|---|
| **Investment risk** | The risk that the underlying investments selected by the customer don't perform as expected, resulting in a reduced value available to provide income in retirement. The two key issues are the actual volatility of the returns over time and the sequence of the returns.<br><br>When a customer withdraws funds the sequence is vitally important as a poor return in the early years combined with a withdrawal will be very difficult to recover.<br>Although it is a simple concept, sequence risk is usually ignored by many members and advisers as they take income from an invested fund rather than isolate the income requirement. This is discussed in more detail later. | Invest in multi-asset funds to diversify risk in the investment portfolio. Some SIPP wrappers also provide access to funds that offer guaranteed capital protection at different points in time to help manage the risk of falling investment markets.<br><br>Purchase a combination of a lifetime or fixed-term annuity to secure the income needed. By purchasing the income at outset the member mitigates sequence risk as their investments will be held for the duration with no withdrawals. Therefore in a period of low or negative returns the fund is not further depleted by an income withdrawal. |
| **Inflation risk** | The risk that the rising costs of goods and services grows faster than income. | Maintain a proportion of DB benefits or purchase an inflation linked annuity with a portion of their fund, combined with the state pension to ensure income keeps pace with essential outgoings. |
| **Change of circumstances risk** | People are living longer in retirement, so it is unreasonable to assume that their circumstances will not change. Typically, they may be widowed, divorced or marry again. They may suffer unforeseen health problems. Some retirement products are restrictive and don't permit changes. | A portfolio of different retirement options may be appropriate and could be designed to provide a combination of certainty and flexibility for the future. |

| Risk | Description | Potential mitigation actions |
|---|---|---|
| **Statutory/ regulatory risk** | The risk that future governments responding to different demographic, social, political or economic situations change the laws or regulations regarding pensions. The previous 20 years is a clear demonstration of how significant this risk can be. | In practice, there is little that can be done to mitigate this risk. Income to cover essential outgoings for life could be secured by either accepting the DB benefits or purchasing a lifetime annuity. |

The risks are real and significant but they can be mitigated with the right guidance and advice. The complexity involved means that members need to be guided to advisers who are experienced in retirement planning and still look to secure essential income and provide a blend of solutions for their clients to diversify the risks they face. Conducting this form of due diligence and adviser selection is a complex task for members and there is likely to be an increasing expectation that their scheme trustees or employer will conduct this exercise on their behalf.

**Employee Risks**  123

## Investments and sequence risk or the danger of taking money out of your retirement fund at the wrong time

This chart uses hypothetical case studies to compare the actual experiences of two people (John and Paul) against the original projections and assumptions that their financial adviser used to plan the level of income that the pension investment would provide in retirement. Although the actual returns for both John and Paul deliver *average* annual growth of 4 per cent over the long term, the sequence of the returns and hence the ultimate outcome, is significantly different.

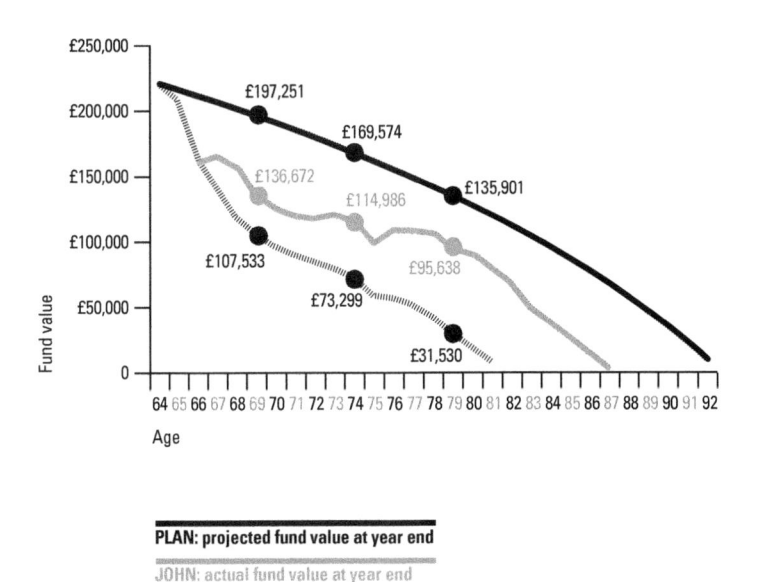

**PLAN: projected fund value at year end**
JOHN: actual fund value at year end
**PAUL: actual fund value at year end**

Notes
Initial drawdown investment: £220,000
Annual income: £12,500
Plan assumes an annual investment growth rate of 4% providing an income of £12,500 a year from age 65 through to age 93, at which point the investment would be exhausted.

## Risk Management

The data in this table details the actual returns and helps clarify the outcomes.

| Age | Plan Annual growth rate (net) | John's actual growth rate (net) | Paul's actual growth rate (net) | Age | Plan Annual growth rate (net) | John's actual growth rate (net) | Paul's actual growth rate (net) |
|---|---|---|---|---|---|---|---|
| 65 | 4.00% | 0.30% | 0.30% | 82 | 4.00% | 1.60% | 1.60% |
| 66 | 4.00% | −17.80% | −17.80% | 83 | 4.00% | −7.50% | 12.20% |
| 67 | 4.00% | 12.20% | −7.50% | 84 | 4.00% | 7.40% | 7.40% |
| 68 | 4.00% | 2.10% | −5.50% | 85 | 4.00% | 5.10% | 5.10% |
| 69 | 4.00% | −5.50% | 2.10% | 86 | 4.00% | −5.50% | −5.50% |
| 70 | 4.00% | 1.60% | 1.60% | 87 | 4.00% | 4.00% | 4.00% |
| 71 | 4.00% | 5.70% | 5.70% | 88 | 4.00% | −5.40% | −5.40% |
| 72 | 4.00% | 10.40% | 10.40% | 89 | 4.00% | 4.80% | 4.80% |
| 73 | 4.00% | 13.20% | 13.20% | 90 | 4.00% | 15.40% | 15.40% |
| 74 | 4.00% | 6.60% | 6.60% | 91 | 4.00% | −5.20% | −5.20% |
| 75 | 4.00% | −2.00% | −2.00% | 92 | 4.00% | 9.00% | 9.00% |
| 76 | 4.00% | 24.90% | 24.90% | 93 | 4.00% | 8.00% | 8.00% |
| 77 | 4.00% | 13.10% | 13.10% | | | | |
| 78 | 4.00% | 8.80% | 8.80% | | | | |
| 79 | 4.00% | 2.10% | 2.10% | | | | |
| 80 | 4.00% | 9.30% | 9.30% | | | Arithmetic average | |
| 81 | 4.00% | −0.70% | −0.70% | | 4.00% | 4.00% | 4.00% |

## Timing is key

The crucial point is that, while the overall average annualized returns are the same in each case, the sequence of the individual annual rates of growth actually achieved, combined with the timing of the income payments taken, has a profound impact. Despite achieving the overall planned average return of 4 per cent , neither investment was actually able to support income payments for as long as projected.

The message illustrated here is that when in drawdown, the *order* in which returns occur is perhaps more important than the average return over a period of time. Recognizing and making plans to mitigate this risk can be key to achieving the desired retirement outcome.

As the Head of Distribution, Steve Lewis is a member of the LV= Retirement Solutions leadership team that has transformed the business over the last 5 years from being a niche annuity provider to a mainstream retirement business. The delivery of new propositions to market has been a key focus of his work, particularly through the transformation of the market resulting from the introduction of pension freedoms. LV= has been at the forefront of technology developments, providing client education and adviser support tools, and now launching groundbreaking on-line education and advice tools. Steve is a retirement specialist with considerable Industry experience, working closely with advisers and providers in the market. To find out more about LV= Corporate Solutions and how they can help you, call the LV= Corporate Solutions team on 08000 850 260, email Corporate.Solutions@lv.com or visit LV.com/corporatesolutions

# PART SEVEN
# Investment strategy

## Dean Wetton Advisory

## Is there such a thing as too much freedom?

The Pandora's Box of choices opened up to pension scheme members makes it very difficult for scheme providers to cater for all the options.

If members take the cash option, scheme governors must maximise returns in the limited time before withdrawal. Yet for those who want an annuity or retirement income, the risk-return ratio must be weighted to ensure a consistent income flow.

Mastertrusts have the built-in structure to deal with the conflicting demands of scheme members. They have the versatility to cater for different levels of administrative control, investment risk exposure and flexibility on withdrawals.

DWA has become the expert on advising employers on Mastertrust solutions for auto-enrolment. Speak to them today.

www.deanwettonadvisory.com

# De-risking investments

## 7.1

*Old orthodoxies about how to manage funds close to retirement are changing, reports Dean Wetton.*

For savers in defined contribution schemes, the world has changed. They can access some or all of their funds from age 55, effectively ending the requirement to purchase an annuity at before age 75. They can now access their pension 25 per cent tax free cash in tranches instead of in one lump sum at the point of retirement. They can now leave their residual pension savings tax free to their dependents.

## So what are the investment implications of the regulatory changes?

The previous orthodoxy was that savers should take higher investment risk in the 'accumulation phase' and then 'de-risk' in the 5–15 years before their expected retirement into 25 per cent cash and the balance in bonds to reduce risk relative to their purchase of an annuity. The expected retirement age was 65–68 either determined by the employer or the state pension age. Usually at least 85 per cent of people are in the 'default strategy' – they have either actively selected it or made no selection, in which case this is the default investment strategy. It is this strategy that we focus on rather than strategies or fund selected by members.

## Investment time frame

Investment problems are relatively easier when there is a clear timeframe, take your mortgage as an example. However, the pension freedom changes mean that people have the freedom to draw their funds from age 55 or (more likely) continue saving until closer to age 75 – that's a 20-year window!

Research from the Pensions Policy Institute looked at when people expect to retire. The results clearly show that very few individuals have a clear idea of when they are going to retire.

## Investment Strategy

### Do people know when they will retire?

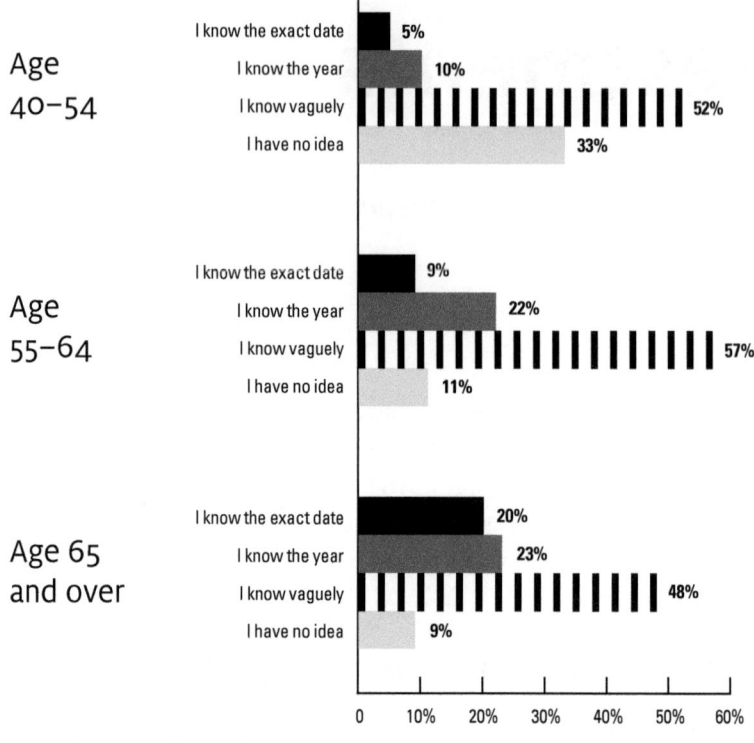

**Age 40–54**
- I know the exact date: 5%
- I know the year: 10%
- I know vaguely: 52%
- I have no idea: 33%

**Age 55–64**
- I know the exact date: 9%
- I know the year: 22%
- I know vaguely: 57%
- I have no idea: 11%

**Age 65 and over**
- I know the exact date: 20%
- I know the year: 23%
- I know vaguely: 48%
- I have no idea: 9%

Source: Pensions Policy Institute

If you don't know when you retire it makes little sense to de-risk into defensive assets at an arbitrary age. It makes more sense to maintain growth by keeping your assets in a diversified portfolio until retirement becomes more certain. Maintaining the old policy exposes members to the risk of having too little growth.

## Members want last-minute decisions

The second Pensions Policy Institute survey looked at when individuals thought they would be best placed to decide how to use their pension pot. Again the results are striking only 12 per cent thought they could do this in their mid-fifties when traditional strategies normally de-risk, while 77 per cent thought they would be best placed only a few years from retirement. With people not wishing to decide on how to use their retirement pot until very close to retirement it follows that it may now be appropriate to keep funds in a well-diversified (multi-asset) portfolio for much longer than was the case before the reforms.

## Point at which respondents believe that they will be best-placed to decide how to use their pension pot

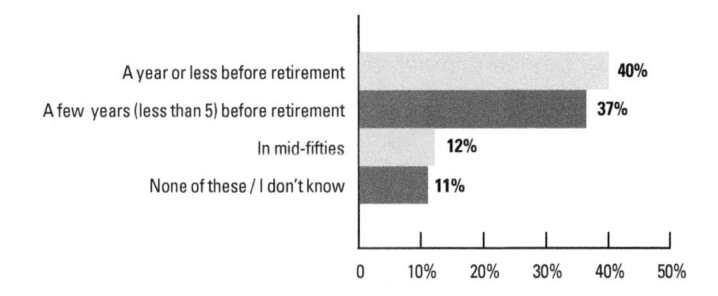

- A year or less before retirement: 40%
- A few years (less than 5) before retirement: 37%
- In mid-fifties: 12%
- None of these / I don't know: 11%

# What are members going to do with their pension pots?

Another part of the Pension Policy Institute survey looked at what individuals intend to do with their pension pot when they retire. The results of this survey provide perhaps the most compelling argument not to automatically de-risk relative to annuity purchase as only 18 per cent plan to buy an annuity. (Other survey results vary but are always a significant minority circa 20 per cent ) In contrast to the media reports, as few as 8 per cent intend to spend this on (say) a Lamborghini. Almost two-thirds want to keep the money invested either in a pension or within another savings vehicle. With such a high proportion it would not seem appropriate for schemes to automatically de-risk significantly in the run-up to retirement.

## What respondents intend to do with the majority of their pension plot

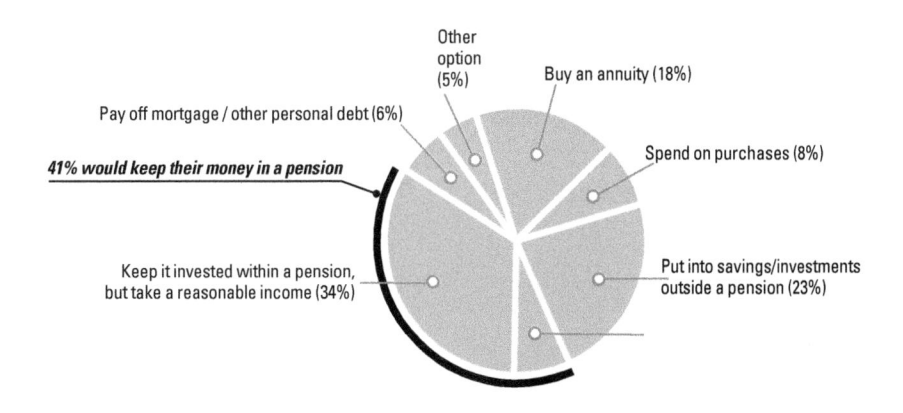

- Other option (5%)
- Buy an annuity (18%)
- Spend on purchases (8%)
- Put into savings/investments outside a pension (23%)
- Keep it invested within a pension, but take a reasonable income (34%)
- Pay off mortgage / other personal debt (6%)

**41% would keep their money in a pension**

## How to reduce risk and maintain growth

When analysing the data DWA have concluded that whether you look at the absolute risk of de-risking a portfolio in advance the full range of retirement choices or whether you are definitely looking to buy an annuity, there are significant risks associated with de-risking into cash and bonds too soon. DWA have also concluded that it is possible to achieve higher returns without taking on significant risk by remaining invested in a well-diversified multi-asset portfolio for longer.

## Accessing retirement income

When considering the default strategy it is also important to consider how members might access retirement income. Few schemes other than mastertrusts are considering in scheme retirement income options. Where in scheme retirement income is offered it makes sense for the default strategy to at least be compatible to reduce transition cost to make for a smooth transition. If out of scheme retirement income is to be offered, is a preferred provider selected or it is simply 'anywhere but here'? We suggest the former approach is likely to improve member outcomes as this will be a difficult choice faced by members.

> Dean Wetton Advisory Limited is a boutique pensions and investment advisory firm founded in 2009 with some £15bn assets under advice and a global client base. Dean Wetton Advisory Limited is an appointed representative of Red Sky Capital LLP which is authorized and regulated by the FCA. For further information, please visit www.deanwettonadvisory.com

# Investments and assets

**7.2**

*Dean Wetton reports on how funds and assets are evolving to meet the expectations of employees.*

There is now a widely shared concern that without appropriate action, pension outcomes in the future will not match members' expectations. In one 2011 survey of DC industry professionals, 70 per cent said that they did not think that scheme members would achieve good outcomes at retirement.

Active governance means ensuring that scheme has a goal for the members, and that the default is managed with this goal in mind. The danger is that members have no goal, or that they are guided towards an inappropriate goal.

It is mandatory for all DC schemes to review their statement of investment principles regularly according to the Pensions Regulator. However according to the Regulator's own survey in 2011, 48 per cent of schemes had not carried out a review in over two years

There are a range of goals that could be set in a scheme. A goal could define the type of assets that are needed at the point of retirement, for example to buy an annuity. Or a goal could define what income in retirement a member is trying to achieve. Goals could also be set with reference to benchmarks such as inflation or stock market indexes, or according to certain risk levels.

These goals require more than just occasional review. In order to optimize their pensions outcome, members should actively make changes in the nature of their portfolio at key moments in their DC savings journey.

Many members are not doing this. A large proportion of DC scheme members are invested in the same fund for the full period of their pension accumulation. One DC industry analyst has estimated that 50 per cent -60 per cent of members in schemes with less than 250 members are invested in this way. It is considered likely that most of these members are in equity-only funds and this would seem evidence of there being no goal in place.

It is evident that members themselves cannot be expected to recognise, let alone rectify their lack of a pensions related goal. This is becoming even more true as DC scheme membership is widened through auto enrolment. So the duty falls on decision makers through active governance to introduce processes by which DC scheme members are de-risked in advance of retirement to ensure that they are not exposed.

'Lifecycling' aims to achieve appropriate changes in the nature of DC scheme members' portfolios in a default fund structure. It separates a growth phase from a de-risking phase, and ensures that members, usually 5-10 years before retirement, are de-risked according to a preset formula which switches them into lower risk asset classes in preparation for retirement.

Lifecycling has weaknesses in relation to goals. It is too mechanistic and inflexible, some say. Another criticism is that its uniform and one-size-fits-all approach does not suit some members. For example, following the ending of compulsory annuitization, a proportion of members may be in a position to take advantage of a flexible drawdown facility at retirement. Their investment objective and risk appetite in the period before retirement will be quite different.

There are emerging forms of default fund which offer solutions to this goal-setting problem. For example there are special kinds of 'target retirement' funds which are each aimed at a different objective, so that members can select either the purchase of an annuity as their objective, or they can set their retirement goal as being to remain in drawdown.

One goal is to maximise a member's assets at retirement, but another and possibly more appropriate one is to help members achieve a desired level of retirement income. With this objective in mind, 'outcome-oriented' default structures offer each member the ability to set a particular income-in- retirement goal, and then for each member to be provided an investment approach which is geared to this goal. This mimics the approach now well established among DB schemes to set the investment goal according to the liabilities of the fund (Liability Driven Investment - LDI).

## Asset allocation

A key aspect of governance in DC is actively enabling members' asset allocation to be 'dynamically' adjusted as may be required from time to time, particularly in the default option. The danger is that scheme members are exposed to too great an extent to stock market volatility, and do not benefit from appropriate asset allocation during the accumulation of their pension savings, and thus suffer from lower than hoped for pension outcomes.

The Pensions Regulator requires that DC decision makers give thought to managing risk to achieve the best outcome for members. It advises that 'the default option's investment strategy should manage these risks through the appropriate and diversified allocation of assets'. DC decision makers must review the design of their scheme's default fund every three years.

Asset allocation can account for between 33 per cent and 75 per cent in the variance of a fund's return, according to recent research (Roger G Ibbotson, The importance of asset allocation, Financial Analysts Journal, Vol 66, No 2, 18–20, 2010). This conclusion applies with particular force to one type of portfolio in particular: long-only passive (or index tracking) investments.

In other words if a passive investment portfolio suffers from a 'set and forget' approach where it is not adjusted actively according to market conditions, then its performance, and member outcomes, may suffer.

Since many DC schemes are significantly weighted towards long- only and passive vehicles, Ibbotson's conclusion offers important supporting evidence for an active approach to asset allocation in DC. So, the best result for members will be achieved if asset allocation is dynamic, by which we mean that it is reviewed frequently, and then changed as appropriate according to market circumstances.

Most lifecycle structures are not dynamic. Members are placed into a predetermined combination of funds that varies according to their age or proximity to retirement, but this predetermined combination may have been set several years before and in quite different market conditions, and anyway relies heavily on members communicating any changes in their planned retirement dates.

DC scheme decision makers seeking an active and dynamic approach to asset allocation, but recognizing that they have neither the time nor the skills to make the necessary changes themselves, can select from a range of external solutions which have become available in recent years.

Diversified growth funds, absolute return funds and other multi- asset vehicles allow the manager of the fund to take immediate and appropriate action with no need to seek the approval of scheme members or trustees. As a result they are increasingly popular within default fund structures, and by 2012 represented 14 per cent of assets in the growth phase of larger company default funds today, according to a survey by DCisions (Calibrating DC Outcomes).

Another way of enabling active asset allocation is by employing target date funds, which are managed dynamically to adapt to market conditions, whilst always being focused on the overall objective of gradually shifting toward a more conservative mix of assets as the fund's specific target retirement date approaches.

Active asset allocation of the sort we are describing here does not necessarily require the use of active investments. We are now seeing the development of multi-asset vehicles built on passive fund building blocks, which are managed actively to adjust asset allocation to meet predetermined targets.

Dean Wetton Advisory Limited is a boutique pensions and investment advisory firm founded in 2009 with some £15bn assets under advice and a global client base. Dean Wetton Advisory Limited is an appointed representative of Red Sky Capital LLP which is authorized and regulated by the FCA. For further information, please visit www.deanwettonadvisory.com

# Performance and value

## 7.3

*Dean Wetton discusses how funds can be held to account.*

**DC** governance should be active in another sense: it should involve a regular review of investment performance relative to the schemes goals. One of the dangers to member outcomes is that the investment managers looking after the scheme assets do not perform well. This is the manager risk.

The Pension Regulator suggests that 'performance of the funds within the default option should ... be checked informally at regular intervals throughout the year'. The Investment Governance Group recommends that DC decision makers should 'regularly assess the performance of each investment option, and the constituent components of the default strategy, against its stated performance objectives'.

Some would counter that decisions in setting objectives, managing risks, allocating assets and engaging members are more important than how a fund performs against a benchmark. Of course such governance considerations are important, but regular investment performance measurement should not be ignored altogether. In many DC schemes, particularly smaller ones, it is possible that this is indeed what is happening.

Even larger and well-advised schemes find selecting appropriate performance measures a challenge. Active governance ensures that managers are measured against benchmarks that are relevant to a scheme's objectives. There is no need to know how a fund has performed relative to the stock market when what might matter is whether it has maintained its value against inflation, for example. Less active decision makers who do not insist on relevant measures may find themselves having to rely on benchmarks which suit the needs and perspective of the manager but not of their scheme.

Even comparing the performance of funds to each other can be difficult. Funds such as diversified growth funds, absolute return and other multi-asset funds, are not one class but a wide array of different approaches that cover a number of categories of fund, seeking to perform against a wide variety of types of benchmark. Comparable performance on a like-for-like basis can be difficult to establish. No wonder that one DC industry service provider says that 'the DC market is flooded with different multi-asset products and there is no method to benchmark them effectively'.

There are solutions to these performance measurement challenges. A common DC benchmark has been developed by DCisions which defines risk objectively and determines whether actual risk experienced has been adequately rewarded. This is consistent with another governance recommendation that 'the key measure of service quality in DC can only be to look at how well members have been rewarded for the risk taken with their money'.

It is possible to avoid the pitfalls in making relevant assessment of performance, by using careful quantitative comparisons combined with qualitative observations of manager processes and systems. The in depth expertise can be developed internally or outsourced but the results should be used to assess performance regularly.

The next step is to take appropriate action where investment performance is not as expected. Replacing one manager for another has been difficult in some DC scheme structures in the past, but is increasingly being made easier by use of white labelled funds which minimize the difficulty for scheme decision makers and members alike in switching from one manager to another.

## Value for money

Schemes should be active in tackling another major threat to outcomes: poor value for money for scheme members. Over 50 per cent of DC decision makers polled by the Pensions Regulator in 2011 revealed confusion or ignorance about of the levels of costs borne by their scheme members. This is hardly surprising, since costs have in the past been presented to decision makers and members alike in ways that are difficult to understand.

The reality is that costs borne by members and sponsors in DC schemes fall under one of three headings: investment, administration and advice. Often these costs are bundled together into one figure, which is what makes them difficult to interpret.

Some schemes, usually larger ones, are willing to subsidize members by paying for both the administration and the advice (for example for the design of the best default fund). This subsidy, combined with astute use of purchasing power to reduce investment fees, explains why some members, typically those in larger schemes, receive such good value DC savings opportunities. However, most companies, especially smaller ones, are not willing or able to subsidize their employees' retirement savings, and require that the members bear the full cost of all three services: investment, administration and advice.

In either event, whether the sponsor subsidizes the member or not, the first task for active DC governance is to be aware of the extent of each of these three costs and what is driving them. This is echoed by the words of the Pensions Regulator – that 'transparency and communication on the level and the structure of charges needs to be of a high standard'. This task was made simpler with the arrival of the new 'RDR' regulations in 2013. Certain costs relating to investment advice will become transparently visible in a way that in the past they were not.

The next task for DC decision makers is then to ensure that services being paid for by members (or by the sponsor) do indeed deliver the expected benefits.

The first of our three cost elements is investment, the fees for which vary according to style of management. More complex funds, for example diversified growth funds, absolute return and other multi- asset funds vehicles charge more than simpler passive funds, but in return they can offer real benefits. Analysis of DC default fund performance by DCision in 2012 concluded that 'lower priced products, most of which are pure equity trackers, delivered a poorer risk/return balance than the higher charging funds'.

It is a common mistake to focus only on investment related cost. In fact the majority of cost borne by members in smaller schemes comes from a combination of the other two costs: administration and advisory fees. (Smaller schemes are important because they represent a large proportion of DC schemes and assets).

In a typical smaller scheme, these two elements can represent two thirds of all the costs borne by the member. Hardly surprising then that in a Pensions Regulator survey of Trust-based DC schemes, 40 per cent of smaller schemes expressed either a lack of confidence or ignorance as to whether the charges incurred by members represented value for money, while only half as many larger schemes expressed such doubts.

The value delivered to members and sponsors by administration activity can be measured in a variety of ways against the efficiency and accuracy of the platform supplier. Actively governed schemes will carry out regular checks on this.

The value delivered by advisers is more difficult to measure, but as it is often the largest single element of cost borne by members, it should be regularly scrutinized. Usually the larger investment and employee benefits consultants charge their fees direct to sponsors, thus members do not pay these costs. But Independent Financial Advisers (IFAs) tend to earn their fees by means of a levy paid for by members, often referred to as commission or 'trail' fee.

In many cases these advice-related fees charged to members can be justified by the one-to-one advisory service offered by their scheme's appointed IFA, but the value to members of any such service should be actively investigated by DC scheme decision makers through regular reviews. Where advisory fees to members are not justified, active DC decision makers should renegotiate them.

The Pensions Regulator has said that 'good value for money does not simply equal low cost'. This echoes best practice in procurement across industry as a whole which suggests that suppliers should indeed not be judged on cost alone. The key advice from the Chartered Institute of Purchasing and Supply (CIPS) is to look at value, quality and continuity of supply, not just price.

Dean Wetton Advisory Limited is a boutique pensions and investment advisory firm founded in 2009 with some £15bn assets under advice and a global client base. Dean Wetton Advisory Limited is an appointed representative of Red Sky Capital LLP which is authorized and regulated by the FCA. For further information, please visit www.deanwettonadvisory.com

# VAT recovery

## 7.4

*HMRC has reconsidered recovery of VAT on pension scheme costs. Are you losing out, asks Elmer Doonan at Dentons.*

As any employer knows, VAT that cannot be recovered represents a significant business cost. One aspect of pension scheme costs where VAT has traditionally not been recoverable is pension fund investment management services. Research by the Pensions Regulator in 2013 indicated that pension fund investment costs represented, on average, between 20 per cent and 27 per cent of total scheme running costs for most schemes and can be over 40 per cent of total running costs for a large pension scheme. Two recent decisions of the Court of Justice of the European Union (CJEU), PPG Holdings BV (C26/12) and ATP Pension Services AS (C464/12), have forced HMRC to review the entire subject of the recovery of VAT on pension scheme costs. It has issued guidance on this and it would pay employers to take account of this to maximise VAT recoveries and in the case of employers who have defined contribution arrangements to recover VAT that may have been paid in error.

Prior to the CJEU cases HMRC permitted sponsoring employers of pension schemes to recover VAT on administration services but not on investment management services. Thus, VAT on professional and pension administration costs were recoverable but VAT on investment management costs were not. In cases where a service provider's invoice included both administrative and investment services, HMRC allowed the recovery of VAT on 30 per cent of the invoice (the 70/30 rule) but the remaining 70 per cent was considered as relating to investment services, so the VAT on it was not recoverable.

## Defined benefit (DB) schemes

In the PPG case the CJEU ruled that where an employer had under legal requirements set up a separate pension fund for its employees it could, as a general rule, recover VAT on services relating to the management of the fund. The case drew no distinction between administrative and investment management costs but it indicated that there should be a direct and immediate link between those services and the employer's economic activities. The effect of this decision was to put previous HMRC practices on VAT recovery in pension schemes in question and it resulted in HMRC issuing four Revenue & Customs Briefs (RCBs) in quick succession, and a fifth brief in October 2015 setting out options for employers to recover the VAT on pension fund management costs in DB schemes. Whilst these recognise the right to recover VAT on investment management costs they will require an employer to set up specific legal structures to ensure that the VAT is recoverable. The 70/30 rule will be phased out by 1 January 2017 so employers will need to have new arrangements in place by then. In fact, these arrangements should be in place much sooner to recover VAT on investment management costs that is now being incurred.

HMRC's guidance on recovering VAT on pension management costs does not distinguish between pension administration costs and investment management costs. It's guidance sets out the new arrangements HMRC will accept. These seems to focus on the need for an immediate and direct link between the employer and the supplier of services to the scheme. At present, three arrangements have been put forward and it is possible more may follow:

## Tripartite agreements

HMRC has confirmed that an employer who enters a tripartite agreement with the trustee and the third party supplier can recover VAT for those services. An employer can use a tripartite agreement to demonstrate that it is the recipient of the supply of fund management services and reclaim VAT if:

- the supplier 'makes its supplies to the employer' and could be appointed by the trustee on behalf of the employer
- the employer pays directly for the services supplied under the contract and not through the scheme
- the supplier will pursue the employer alone for payment and only seek to recover them from the trustee where the employer is unable to pay (for example, insolvency)
- both the trustee and the employer can make claims against the provider for breach of contract
- the supplier agrees to provide fund performance reports to the employer on request, subject to certain special circumstances
- the employer has power to terminate the contract (although this could be subject to trustee consent)

One difficulty with tripartite agreements is that a third party supplier may be reluctant to enter the arrangement since it is likely to deviate from its standard terms.

It remains to be seen whether fund managers will recognise the need to adjust their terms to recognise the VAT issues.

## Supply of pension scheme administration services by trustee to an employer

This will involve the trustee contracting with and paying third party service providers and then, separately, contracting with the employer to provide to the employer the service of running the pension scheme (including asset management services) on the employer's behalf. In effect, the trustee will have sub-contracted its obligations to the employer to the supplier. VAT paid by the employer on the services of the trustee, and services supplied by the supplier to the trustee will be recoverable. This option may not be suitable to all schemes but it is one way that might avoid problems involved in tripartite agreements.

## VAT grouping

A corporate trustee may be able to join an employer's existing VAT grouping so that supplies made to the trustee in dealing with the assets of the pension scheme are treated as made to a representative member of the VAT group. HMRC has said that it will not seek to recover any VAT debt of the VAT group from the pension scheme assets unless that VAT debt is attributable to the pension scheme. Obviously, this option is limited to corporate trustees but if it works for an employer the costs and benefits of establishing a corporate trustee may make this a worthwhile step.

## Defined contribution schemes

In the ATP Pension Service case the CJEU decided that defined contribution (DC) pension schemes were within the definition of 'special investment funds' in Article 13B(d)(6) of the Sixth Council Directive on VAT and which exempts their management from VAT. HMRC accepts that this means DC schemes are exempt from VAT on investment management services and, possibly, some administration services. HMRC's guidance issued in November 2014 sets out some conditions that must be met to qualify for the exemption:

- They are solely funded (whether directly or indirectly) by persons to whom the retirement benefit is to be paid. This ought to include both employer and

employee contributions on the basis that the former are an entitlement of the employee.
- The pension customer bears the investment risk. DC schemes with a DB underpin may not qualify.
- The fund contains the pooled contributions of several pension customers.
- The risk borne by the customers is spread over a range of securities.

Whilst most DC schemes should meet these conditions it will be necessary to examine the terms and the operation of the scheme to ensure that it qualifies.

It is likely that employers have wrongly paid VAT on investment management services for their DC scheme in the past. Immediate steps ought to be taken to ensure no further VAT is charged and to recover VAT paid in error. The latter will be limited to VAT paid in the 4 years prior to the claim. If the investment manager is UK-based it should be asked to recover the VAT and to refund it to the trustee. If the investment manager is based overseas then the trustee will need to recover the VAT from HMRC.

Elmer Doonan is a Partner and head of pensions in Dentons London office. Dentons is the world's largest law firm providing tailored solutions to meet the local, national and global needs of clients in 125 locations in over 50 countries. Telephone 02072467151 E-mail: elmer.doonan@dentons.com; www.dentons.com

# IoD

## "For me, it's about high-calibre connections."

"I've been with the IoD for almost ten years. Through my membership I have the opportunity of meeting senior, experienced and inspiring people across all sectors. We learn, we engage and share ideas with each other. We face the same challenges, the same pressures – we have the same questions – and I believe together we stand a better chance of surviving times like these. I get to have conversations I wouldn't ordinarily have, with the space and amenities that impress, plus a host of extras from legal and tax advice, to great events. Do I think it's a good idea to join the IoD? It's a no-brainer – it's invaluable."

**Jason Choy**, Welcome Gate
Member since 2002

### IoD Membership provides:

Free access to IoD meeting space • Local networking events across the UK • Free one-to-one business advice • National conferences, seminars and events • Free business information and research • Free business tax and legal advice • Your views represented to Government • Exclusive online networking

To find out more about the benefits of membership visit
**www.iod.com/benefits**

**Not a member of the IoD?** To apply for membership, or for more information, please call **020 7766 8888** or visit **www.iod.com**

# INDEX OF ADVERTISERS

| | |
|---|---|
| Arc Benefits | 20 |
| BWCI | 56 |
| Dean Wetton | 126 |
| Dentons | *opposite Contents page* |
| Institute of Directors | 142 |
| LV= Corporate Solutions | 74 |
| PTL | 106 |
| Rothesay Life | 68 |